God, Me &
a Cup of Tea
for the Seasons

101 devotional readings to savor
during your time with God

Michele Huey

Michele Huey
www.michelehuey.com

First Edition
ISBN-13: 978-1727281903
ISBN-10: 172728190X

Book Layout © 2018 BookDesignTemplates.com

Printed in the United States of America

To My Grandchildren
Brent, Alex, Madison, Kyle, Deagen,
Delaney, Ben, Joe, Ava

To everything there is a season.

–Ecclesiastes 3:1 NKJV

Contents

To the Reader

I'M NOT A HOLIDAY freak. The only times I decorate my house for the season are in the fall (my favorite season) and for Christmas. But I relish and savor every season of the year, with changing skies, weather, and reasons to celebrate life. From the freshness of the New Year—with its rekindled hopes, renewed dreams, reignited purposes—to decking the house with evergreen boughs and setting Christmas candles in the windows, each day brings with it new challenges and a fresh start.

The devotional readings in this book are a compilation of the newspaper columns I've written over the past twenty-one years. Hence, you may notice a recurrence of certain themes and anecdotes. It is my prayer that reading each one will evoke your own memories, and you will see in your own life the abiding presence, abundant provision, and able protection of a God who loves you more than you can fathom.

In addition, I've sprinkled in a few poems and brief personal experience stories. You have my permission to use anything in this book in holiday programs and publications, as long as you include my name as the author and the following permission and copyright information: "From *God, Me & a Cup of Tea for the Seasons* by Michele Huey, © 2018 Michele Huey. All rights reserved. Used with permission. Visit Michele's website www.michelehuey.com."

Please note the first set of Advent readings are grouped so you can use them when you light the Advent candles each week.

So, brew that cup of tea, grab your Bible, and head for your quiet place. God is waiting. Selah!

Blessings,
Michele
August 2018

New Year's Day

My Presence will go with you.

–Exodus 33:14 NIV

Grandma's Quilts

"For I know the plans I have for you," declares the LORD, "plans to prosper you and not to harm you, plans to give you hope and a future."
–Jeremiah 29:11 NIV

I RECEIVED MY FIRST patchwork quilt as a Christmas gift from my husband's grandmother over thirty years ago.

Grandma loved to make quilts. She'd spend the year gathering discarded clothing, cutting the square patches, then piecing together a mix-match of colors, patterns, and fabrics. Over the years everyone in the family had received at least one of her patchwork quilts. And none of the quilts was the same. Each was one of a kind.

Grandma's quilts weren't masterpieces to be displayed at fairs, bought for a high price, only to hang on someone's quilt rack, unused, because they were too beautiful for daily wear and tear, the countless washing and drying that would leave them faded and worn.

No, Grandma's quilts were made to be used. We used ours— as both bedspread and blanket in both our home and our camper. They served as warm wrappers at early spring baseball games and as seat cushions on hard, sometimes rough bleachers. And when they were beginning to show wear and tear, they still had plenty of use left in them as picnic or beach blankets.

Grandma's quilts weren't delicate, falling apart after only a few years of use. After thirty years, I still have a few around, and in they're still in good condition. My grandchildren use them for sleepovers.

But Grandma's quilts serve more than a physical need. They are a symbol of life itself.

First, they remind me that recycling is an important part of life. And not just recycling of paper and glass and cans. But of plans and hopes and dreams. Very few things in life turn out the way we plan. But we can go on because we can take those discards and reshape and rearrange them for a new purpose.

Second, the patchwork reminds me that an all-light canvas has no contrast, no depth. The dark times in our lives teach us compassion, humility, and persistence, and strengthen faith and trust. Without pain and trouble, we would be shallow persons indeed.

Third, the quilts remind me that it's okay to be "common." I'd rather be an everyday vessel in the hand of God than a treasure of beauty set on a shelf, admired but unused.

Finally, just as each quilt is unique, each life is unique, planned and pieced together with threads of love woven and designed by the Master, God Himself.

Dear God, thank you for being the Master Quiltsman of my life. Thank you for the way You piece together dark and light, rough and smooth, solid and patterned, plain and showy, for a unique creation to be used for Your glory. Amen.

MORE TEA: Read and meditate on Lamentations 3:21–26.

Quilting

Discarded dreams,
like clothes that no longer fit,
bagged up,
put away
in the attic of yesterday.

Colors faded,
seams softly strained
from the weight
of a thousand life-cares;
wrinkled, tired, shapeless now,
these dreams that were mine.

But make them over
to warm the cold night.
In patches of color,
blend dark squares with bright.
Old dreams, like old clothes,
reshaped, rearranged,
can be used once again.

Selah!

Selah! –Psalm 46: 3, 7, 11 NIV

IF I WERE TO choose a Scripture to describe my life in 2017, I'd select Psalm 46. The psalm begins, "God is our refuge and strength, an ever-present help in trouble." The year was filled with many challenges, particularly health issues and family transitions.

If I were to choose a Scripture for the New Year—as a theme verse to reflect on throughout the year—I'd select a word used seventy-four times in the Bible (mostly in Psalms) and often overlooked. Perhaps we ignore it because it's only one little word of five letters standing all by itself at the end of a verse. Perhaps we pay little attention to it because no one knows with certainty its meaning, not even biblical scholars. So we skip right over it and keep on reading.

But the word *selah* is not to be ignored, even if we don't know what it means.

Strong's Concordance defines *selah* as "to lift up, to exalt."

So the first word I want to focus on is *praise*.

Sometimes the phrase "Praise God!" slips through our lips almost meaninglessly and is soon forgotten. How often do we truly praise God—from the heart, not just the mouth?

On a drive to my doctor's appointment, I spent nearly the entire forty-five minutes praising God—aloud. It all started when I thanked Him for dry roads and good weather. One praise flowed after another. Once the pump was primed, the water of praise just gushed out.

Too often I focus on my problems, not on praise. Can it really be that much easier to list a litany of laments than all the ways God has lavished us with His love?

Another definition for *selah* is "the writer's instruction to the reader to pause and exalt the Lord," or "pause and calmly think of that!"

The focus here is on the word *pause*.

How often do we intentionally pause and praise God? I'm ashamed to admit it, but I don't give God the time He is due. Too often my prayer and Bible reading time is like rushing through the drive-through, gobbling junk to appease my hunger, rather than taking the time to savor the banquet and sip from the overflowing cup of blessings my Lord places before me (Psalm 23: 5).

Try it. Put your day on pause and sit down and focus on the things you can praise God for. Little things. Big things. Speak them aloud—there's power in the spoken word—or write them down. It won't be long before the clouds of hopelessness and despair part and you feel the warmth of His sunshine in your soul.

Pause and praise—and one more thing—Presence.

Just as the meaning of *selah* is uncertain, so are the days that will comprise the coming year.

But of one thing I am certain: that His Presence will go with me (Exodus 33:14). For He has promised, "Never will I leave you; never will I forsake you" (Hebrews 13:5; Deuteronomy 31:6).

What is your focus verse for the New Year?

Thank You, Lord, for being with me every moment of every day. Remind me to pause and praise You often throughout the New Year. Amen.

MORE TEA: Read and meditate on Psalm 46.

The Backpack

Come to me, all you who are weary and burdened, and I will give you rest. –Matthew 11:28 NIV

I ONCE BELONGED TO an online prayer group comprised of women in the speaking and writing ministry. One time after I submitted a prayer request for our monthly day of prayer, I received a phone call from one of the members.

"I want to pray with you," she said.

I was surprised and humbled. I didn't think my request warranted a long distance call from a busy woman who I was sure had better things to do.

Afterward, she told me that, while we prayed, she had a vision of a backpack I'd been carrying for a long time. In her vision, Jesus took the backpack from me and put it on Himself. He carried it with Him to Calvary, then to the grave. He still had it when He emerged from the tomb, alive on Easter morning, when He opened it.

"Out came all sorts of beautiful things—butterflies, a loaf of bread," she said. "I don't know if that means anything to you."

It wasn't until later that I understood.

You see, I *do* carry a backpack—not a physical backpack but a spiritual one. Every time I feel a sliver of envy, a spark of anger, or a flicker of discouragement and deny it, I add another stone to my backpack. Because the stones are so small—and because I don't dwell on these negative things—they seem too insignificant to confess to God. But after a while the stones begin to add up and take up space. Eventually the backpack becomes cumbersome and slows me down. But when I confess the stones of envy, anger, and lack of faith, I give them to Jesus, who is waiting to take my load from me.

How heavy a backpack I'd been lugging around! It was time to face my failings and relinquish the load.

A few days later I emailed my friend: "How can I thank you enough for obeying the nudging of the Holy Spirit and phoning me to pray the other day? I realized after I spoke and prayed with you that I put on a good face and don't realize there are hidden hurts buried deep inside: unanswered prayers, disappointments, discouragement. Instead of taking them to God at the first sign, I shove them into the backpack because at that point they're so small and light, I don't think they're important enough to take to God. And envy. Oh, my. A lot of ugly stuff in that backpack. What a beautiful vision of what Jesus does—takes that backpack crammed with all the ugly stuff that, put all together, is far heavier than I'd realized, and transforms it into something beautiful."

What's in your backpack? Why not give it to Jesus and start the New Year off unencumbered by the past? Only He can turn your stones into bread.

Dear God, help me to throw off everything that hinders and the sin that so easily weighs me down, and run with perseverance the race that You have marked out for me (adapted from Hebrews 12:1). Amen.

MORE TEA: Read and meditate on Matthew 11:28–30.

At the Portal of Time

However many years a man may live, let him enjoy them all. –
Ecclesiastes 11:8 NIV

ONCE AGAIN WE STAND at the Portal of Time, the old year
behind us, and, through the door, the New Year.

I'm not one to dwell on the events of the past year. Neither
do I ponder what the New Year will bring. I make plans, but I
know they can be changed in an instant. All I have to do is look
back and I'm reminded that "many are the plans in the mind of
a man, but it is the purpose of the LORD that will be established"
(Proverbs 19:21).

And I'm not one to go through old pictures and scrapbooks. I
used to save greeting cards, but after you've been married for
forty-five years and have lived sixty-seven, the boxes of such
stuff become overwhelming. I think a few pictures, a few mementoes of special events are all that's needed.

It's a mistake to live life in the past, wrote Richard Paul Evans, author of The Walk series. "One cannot ride a horse
backwards and still hold its reins." (Note to readers: If you haven't read The Walk series, I highly recommend it.)

As time goes on, I find I dwell on the good things and process the "bad," learn from it, and move on.

I put quotation marks around the word "bad" because I believe if God is in control of my life, nothing that happens to me is bad. Call me Pollyanna, but I know God can (and will) redeem situations that aren't to my liking.

"Redeem" is a word we hear in church often: With His own blood, Christ redeemed our souls—bought them back from the Evil One.

To redeem, however, means more than "to free from captivity by payment of a ransom." It also means "to make (something that is bad, unpleasant, etc.) better or more acceptable," "to offset the bad effect of, to make worthwhile." (Definitions from the *Merriam-Webster Online Dictionary*)

I love that my God can redeem even the ugliest, most painful situations in my life.

I know there is evil in the world. I shudder when I think of it. But the child of God need not fear evil. "Because you have made the LORD, who is my refuge, even the Most High, your dwelling place, no evil shall befall you . . . for He shall give His angels charge over you, to keep you in all your ways" (Psalm 91:9–11).

I've learned to embrace the high points and low points, times of joy and times of sorrow, times of disappointment, discouragement, and concern, as well as times of high cotton, because God has allowed them all in order to make me what I am, to shape me into the person He wants me to me.

"For I know the plans I have for you," declares the LORD, "plans to prosper you and not to harm you, plans to give you hope and a future" (Jeremiah 29:11).

"Life is not a sprint. It was never meant to be," writes Evans in *A Step of Faith*. "It is just one step of faith after another."

Help me, Father, to learn from the past, embrace the present, and step into the future with faith, knowing that Your Presence will go with me (Exodus 33:14). Amen.

MORE TEA: Read and meditate on Ecclesiastes 3:1–8.

Facing the Future

My Presence will go with you. –Exodus 33:14 NIV

Nothing can separate you from God's love. Nothing in all creation will ever be able to separate us from the love of God that is revealed in Christ Jesus our Lord. –Romans 8:39 NLT

I MUST HAVE HAD my head in a groundhog hole, because I never heard the term "fiscal cliff" before the 2012 election. Then I heard of it or read about it every day. It cast a pall over the New Year and fanned a fear of the future. I'd be amiss to say I didn't feel at least a little anxiety about what 2013 held.

Although we didn't plunge over the cliff, dreams of retirement faded daily. We lived on one income—my husband's—and what little I made writing and editing. Dreams are always bigger than your pocketbook, but it's sure nice to at least hope. The looming specter of the cliff robbed me of hope.

But the problem wasn't the fiscal cliff, it was my perspective. You see, I tend to focus on the wrong thing. When you stare long enough at the mountain, all you see is the mountain, not beyond it.

Rather than focus on fear of the unknown, I need to focus on what I'm sure of and trust to be true: God's love, faithfulness, and presence.

I think often of the Israelites and their journey into the wilderness to the Promised Land, their lack of faith in a God who loved them and had a magnificent plan for them. But they didn't get it. They failed their Savior over and over. In unbelief, they refused to enter the Promised Land when they got there. The punishment for their disobedience was to wander in the wilderness until all of that rebellious generation died.

Yet God did not abandon them. He fed them with manna for forty years until the time came to enter the Promised Land. Even their clothes didn't wear out (Deuteronomy 8:4; 29:5). Yet when they settled in, they were unfaithful and worshiped false gods. After they were taken into exile as punishment, God still did not desert them. Through the prophets He reassured them over and over of His love—an everlasting, steadfast, unconditional love. I think of Daniel, Shadrach, Meshach, and Abednego. God did not abandon them in their land of exile. He prospered them.

Is the world today any different? Rebellion and disobedience abound, as was foretold (see 2 Timothy 3). But God has not changed. He *cannot* change (Malachi 3:6). "If we are faithless, He will remain faithful, for He cannot deny Himself" (2 Timothy 2:13). His love is still steadfast, unfailing, bigger and broader and greater than anything we can imagine. He will never fail us or forsake us (Hebrews 13:5). Even though we may go into a financial exile, He will prosper His faithful ones in ways we cannot imagine.

While the fiscal fears for the New Year may be well founded, so is my faith in God. He is and will always be "my refuge and strength, an ever-present help in time of trouble. Therefore I will not fear" (Psalm 46:1, 2). How about you?

As I enter the unknown of the New Year, Lord God, thank You for reminding me of Your abiding presence, abundant provision, awesome plan, and able protection. Throughout the coming year, open my eyes daily to Your unfailing love and faithfulness. Amen.

MORE TEA: Read and meditate on Romans 8:28–39.

Using a Bible concordance, note Scriptures referring to God's love, faithfulness, and presence.

Banging on the Pots

If anyone is in Christ, he is a new creation; the old has passed away, behold, the new has come. –2 Corinthians 5:17 RSV

GROWING UP, I HAD firm bedtimes, but the one day of the year I was allowed to stay up late was December 31. At midnight we'd usher in the New Year on the front porch, banging on pots and pans.

After I married, new traditions were added: playing board games with family on New Year's Eve, then eating hot dogs and sauerkraut at midnight. On New Year's Day, we'd have dinner—pork roast and sauerkraut, of course—at my in-laws' home, then spend the rest of the day with family.

Somewhere along the line, I began making New Year's resolutions—the same ones every year: lose weight, be on time, remember birthdays and anniversaries, eat right, exercise, set time aside every day for prayer and Bible reading. I figure I've made progress if I can keep them for a week, let alone the entire year!

New Year traditions differ from culture to culture, from country to country, and date as far back as 4,000 years ago, when the ancient Babylonians observed the New Year by returning borrowed farm equipment. As time passed, new customs were added, each believed to affect luck for the coming year: A hog symbolized prosperity, as did cabbage; hence the pork and sauerkraut. Making noise at the stroke of midnight was believed to ward off evil spirits. And the first visitor of the New Year affected the luck of the household for that year. A dark, handsome visitor was believed to bring the best luck.

A brand new year means a brand new start. Another chance to get it right, to do it right. We wish for peace, prosperity, health, and happiness. And at midnight on January 1, our hopes sparkle like the stars in the winter sky.

But we don't have to wait for a new year to erase the mistakes of the past and start anew. God tells us in His Word that, when we accept the gift of His Son as Savior and Lord, we are new creatures (2 Corinthians 5:17), born again, this time spiritually (John 3:3), and our sins are removed from us as far as the east is from the west (Psalm 103:12). And if we make a mistake, all we have to do is tell Him, and He'll forgive and cleanse us (1 John 1:9).

With God in our lives, we have hope year-round. We don't need to bang on pots and pans to ward off evil spirits, for He is a shield around us (Psalm 3:3) and will assign angels to watch over us (Psalm 91:11; 34:7). And when things go wrong, as they eventually will, we don't have to face the bad times alone, for God's presence will go before us into each day (Hebrews 13:5, 6; Exodus 33:14), and we can count on His faithfulness, His promises, and His provision (Matthew 7:7–11). Chance, or luck, is haphazard. God is a rock (Psalm 62:2, 6, 7).

Someone once said that man without God faces a hopeless end, but man with God has an endless hope.

As another year ends and a new one begins, I won't be up, banging on pots and pans or eating pork and sauerkraut at midnight. I'll be sleeping soundly in my bed, resting in the knowledge that my times are in His hands (Psalm 31:15), and there are no better hands than that.

The New Year, Lord, will bring times of sadness and happiness, times to grow in faith, hope, and love. Thank You that I do not need to face these times alone. Thank You for the promise of Your presence, protection, and provision. Amen.

MORE TEA: Read and meditate on Psalm 91.

When Joy Chose Me

Come, let us sing with joy to the LORD. –Psalm 95:1 NIV

AT FIRST I DIDN'T think anything of it. But when the word *joy* jumped out at me time and time again, in different scenarios, I took notice.

The year's challenges had crescendoed into a drumroll, and by December joy was anything but thriving. Normally when someone asks me how I am, I answer, with a hearty smile, "Great!" or "Good!" But lately the best answer I could come up with (without lying) was an anemic "Okay." Accompanied by a pitiful shrug.

What happened to my joy?

Getting snuffed out by the stuff of life, and I was letting it happen.

So when joy jumped out at me repeatedly during December, I sensed God was telling me something: "Choose joy."

I'd thought I was dealing with the stuff of life, but in reality I was really ignoring it, allowing it to bury me. I chose, not joy, but distress, anxiety, fear, and despair.

Joy is a choice.

A wise king once wrote, "However many years a man may live, let him enjoy them all" (Ecclesiastes 11:8). *Enjoy* is a verb. Active, not passive. An action.

The writer of Ecclesiastes tells us to choose joy in all seasons of life. In the good years and the not-so-good years.

How is joy even possible when life is beating you up? How can you smile when your insides are crying?

I saw a poster this morning answering that question: "The reason behind my smile is God."

Choosing joy means embracing all that life encompasses, knowing that "the God on the mountain is still God in the valley. The God of the good times is still God in the bad times. The God of the day is still God in the night" (from "God on the Mountain" by Tracy Dartt).

Choosing joy means choosing to "let your hope keep you joyful, be patient in trouble, and pray at all times" (Romans 12:12).

Choosing joy means choosing to believe God will work things out: "Why are you downcast, O my soul? Why so disturbed within me? Put your hope in God, for I will yet praise Him, my Savior and my God" (Psalm 42:5).

When it came time to select the one word to focus on in the New Year, I didn't have to choose. It had already chosen me: joy.

Thank You, Lord, for opening my eyes to joy. Amen.

MORE TEA: Read and meditate on Psalm 95.

When It Rains

Be strong and courageous. Do not be terrified; do not be discouraged, for the LORD your God will be with you wherever you go. –Joshua 1:9 NIV

OY, WHAT A MONTH! Make that a month and a half. Up until November, 2006 in the Huey household was cruising along, with a few bumps, but cruising nonetheless.

Then November came. One Sunday morning, my husband woke up with his left arm numb. By the end of the week, both hands were numb, as well as his right foot. A trip to the doctor resulted in various medical tests and a referral to a neurologist, who ordered her own tests. MRIs, ultrasounds, CT scans, X-rays, bloodwork—he was tested for everything from sleep apnea to diabetes.

So going into the Christmas season we were already feeling a bit of stress. Then our daughter and her family arrived for their annual Christmas visit. "Christmas with Jaime" was scheduled for the Sunday after she arrived, and I planned for a house-full. So when does life go as you plan?

Two hours after they pulled in, our other two grandchildren, who live next door, came up to play with their cousins, whom they see only once a year. Two hours later, our seven-year-old grandson fell off the back of the couch and broke his elbow—right along the growth plate. After surgery to place two pins in, he was sent home with his arm wrapped in a splint and orders not to bump it. (Right.)

The week wasn't filled with the mother–daughter talks and the grandmother time I looked forward to all year. Illness and injury reigned instead. Our four-year-old granddaughter cried all day Monday with a double ear infection, our two-year-old grandson threw up on the couch, our daughter spent two days in bed with a recurrence of the strep throat that put her down for a week the previous month, and, no sooner was she up and around when her husband fell sick with a nasty stomach virus that was going around.

By the time they left, I was exhausted from the emotions, the stress, and the twenty loads of laundry I did that week. (I do that many in a month for just the two of us.)

But despite all the trauma, I didn't look forward to the end of her visit. I started missing her two days before she left, and when they did pull out, I had this sick feeling in the pit of my stomach. No, not the norovirus, but the usual sadness and loneliness I always feel when we say goodbye.

The bumps, however, didn't end with her departure: the next week the stomach virus made its rounds in our family.

Through it all, I learned a couple things about myself: One, I can't clean up puke like I used to when my kids were little. And, two, even though I'm older and don't have the energy I had when my kids were little, I've learned to lean on the God who never leaves me.

Because when life is out of my control—and isn't it always?—it's never out of His.

Dear God, thank You for reminding me that, although I don't know what the new year will bring, I do know that Your presence will go with me and You will give me rest—rest from fear, worry, and doubt—and You will provide the strength I need to face the mountains I know are ahead. Amen.

MORE TEA: Read and meditate on Joshua 1:1–9.

The Most Important Resolution

*However many years a man may live, let him enjoy them all. —
Ecclesiastes 11:8 NIV*

I CAN'T REMEMBER THE last time my husband and I went out
for New Year's Eve. We usually stay in and watch a movie, and
are sound asleep long before the clock strikes twelve.

But one New Year's Eve, we accepted an invitation to a party
at the home of one of the couples from our Bible study group.
We wondered how on earth we'd ever stay awake until the ball
dropped, but our hosts put our fears to rest with a variety of fun
games.

When we arrived, we each wrote down one of our New Year's
resolutions on a three-by-five card, without including our
names. The cards were then drawn one by one, and we guessed
whose resolution was read.

Pen in hand, I thought about what I'd put down. Exercise?
Lose weight? Get better organized? Keep the finances under
control?

I thought about the year that was ending. I'd tried to lose weight, but I can't say no to pasta, bread, and chocolate.

As far as organization, well, it's coming. I just need to be more ruthless in what I pitch.

And the finances—we're much better off now than we were at this time last year. God has guided, taught, and blessed. Budgeting—before the paychecks come in, not after—really works, as does keeping a spending journal. I even began stashing away two percent of our income for a "Fun Fund" and a "Clothing Fund." We no longer use the credit card to make ends meet, and Christmas was paid for.

What was the one thing I really wanted to work on for the New Year? I thought about my grandchildren and how they love to spend time at our house, playing games with Grandma and just hanging out. Too many times I told them they couldn't come because I was too busy. Or if they did, they'd have to entertain themselves.

Foolish me! The way time flies, it won't be long and they'll be teenagers, not wanting to spend time with me.

I thought about Friday night date night with my hubby. No chores when he comes home from work. "For one evening, you're all mine," I insist. We feast on homemade pizza and watch a movie. He's usually snoring away before the movie is over, but we both look forward to that one night a week when we "make the world go away."

So I wrote, "Have more fun."

Fun times keep us in touch with joy and refill the joy pool depleted by everyday life. Joy and laughter, like gas in the tank, are vital to our running well.

In his book, *The Joys of Successful Aging*, Dr. George Sweeting says that laughter really is good medicine: "Scientists have been studying the effect of laughter on human beings and have found that laughter has a profound and instantaneous effect on virtually every important organ in the human body. Laughter reduces health-sapping tensions and relaxes the tissues as well as exercising the most vital organs. It is said that laughter, even when forced, results in beneficial effects mentally and physically. Next time you feel nervous and jittery, indulge in a good laugh."

God's Word counsels us to be cheerful: not only is it good medicine (Proverbs 17:22), it is a "continual feast" (Proverbs 15:15) and spreads happiness around (Proverbs 15:13). Read the gospels, and you'll find that Jesus Himself took time out for fun, attending weddings and often having dinner with friends.

Frederick Faber once wrote: "There are souls in this world which have the gift of finding joy everywhere and leaving it behind them when they go."

May I be such a soul!

Dear God, remind me every day to have some fun. Amen.

MORE TEA: Read and meditate on Psalm 118.

Valentine's Day

The greatest of these is love.

–1 Corinthians 13:13 NIV

How Does He Love Me?

Rejoice in the wife of your youth. –Proverbs 5:18 RSV

HOW DOES HE LOVE ME? Let me count the ways.

He makes breakfast on Saturday mornings (and Sundays) and cleans up the kitchen, which has usually been neglected for a couple of days, so I can have time to write.

He makes supper after working a twelve-hour day when the pain from my herniated disc has bound me to the loveseat with a heating pad on my back, which is almost every weekday now.

He makes my tea just the way I like it.

He brings in the firewood so we can conserve heating oil and I don't have to be cold. He knows I hate being cold.

He repairs my '97 Explorer in the freezing rain, blowing snow, and frigid temperatures because we need a second vehicle and can't afford a payment on a new one just yet. And because I can't drive the truck anymore—it aggravates my pain.

He spends two hours blowing snow from the lane after supper, in the dark, when he'd rather be working on an inside project or cozied up on the couch watching *NCIS* reruns with me, so I can get out in the morning.

He watches *NCIS* reruns for the *nth* time because it's my favorite program, even if there's something else he's interested in watching (unless it's an elk-hunting show).

He puts down a new floor in the kitchen and kick plates on the cabinets in the evenings after work.

He listens with patience when I whine (or maybe he's just pretending to listen).

He drives me to a speaking engagement near Pittsburgh, a two-plus hour drive one way, on a Monday evening, waits in the Ranger while I speak, then drives me home in still another snowstorm.

He gets up at five a.m. and goes to work the next day, even though we got home after midnight.

He texts me at work to make sure I got there safely.

He doesn't complain when we have leftover leftovers.

He eats everything I make, even when it doesn't turn out. (He once told me, "I was in the service. I can eat anything." Forty-five years later, the statement is still true.)

He doesn't mind the dust, even when it's been around a while (like a month or more).

He vacuums the floor because running the vacuum hurts my back.

He packs his lunch every morning because I don't do lunch buckets. (Besides, every time I do, I get something wrong.)

He supports me in every decision I make, whether or not he agrees with it.

I know it sounds like he's perfect. He's not. But he's perfect for me. He's the Valentine of Valentines, a daily gift from God, my life partner in every sense of the word.

Live happily with the woman you love through all the . . . days of life that God has given you under the sun. The wife God gives you is your reward for your earthly toil (Ecclesiastes 9:9 NLT).

Dear God, thank You for my husband. He is the most unselfish person I know. Help me to be the wife he needs, the wife he deserves. Bless him as he has been a blessing to me—exceedingly abundantly above all he can ask or imagine (Ephesians 3:20). Amen.

MORE TEA: Read and meditate on Ecclesiastes 4:9–12.

The Miracle of Love

Then the LORD God made a woman . . . and he brought her to the man. –Genesis 2:22 NIV

"LOVE IS A MIRACLE," I told my husband after we attended a wedding.

The groom's love for his bride shone from his eyes, was etched in every line of his face as he watched her approach him on her father's arm.

"You must be so in love," I told him after the ceremony.

He beamed. "Oh, I am!"

Love is a miracle. Think of it—one man meets one woman and falls in love—and she loves him in return. What, with all the billions of men and women in the world, are the chances of that? Yet it happens every day.

I remember when I met my husband. I was drawn to him instantly—his gentle manner, his tall, slender frame, his trim beard, and curly, shoulder-length hair—but it was those twinkling blue eyes that did me in.

What a wonder when I found out that he was attracted to me, too! I mean, I was the girl who, in grade school, could never get anyone to "like me back." Who wondered in high school if she'd ever go steady (I did). Who, in college, accepted a proposal from someone she thought was the love of her life, only to have him drop her a year later without an explanation. Who, after having her heart shattered, gave up on love and focused on a career.

And then, three months after vowing never to fall in love again, I met Dean. On our first date I knew deep down, where there are no words, that he was "The One." We married eleven months after we met. The heart, indeed, has a mind of its own.

I still thrill at the sight of him. Time and life, with all the disappointments and curve balls and tests and trials, have only strengthened and deepened the bond we share. And, wonder of wonders, after experiencing me at my worst, he loves me still!

Some call it chemistry. I call it God.

After all, He is love (1 John 4:16). He created woman for man and performed the first marriage ceremony (Genesis 2:18–25; 1 Corinthians 11:8–9) because He knew that "two are better than one" (Ecclesiastes 4:9–12). He blessed us with the gifts of romance and passion, which, within the boundaries He set, are gifts, not sin (Song of Solomon).

Love is a miracle and miracles are matters of the heart, not the head. If you have to talk yourself into loving someone, it isn't love. With love, using your head and all your reasoning ability doesn't work.

The miracle of love. One man. One woman. Loving—and in love with—each other. Wow.

Dear God, thank You for the love that blesses and brightens my life. Amen.

MORE TEA: Read and meditate on Song of Solomon 2:3–13.

To My Husband on Valentine's Day

Let love and faithfulness never leave you; bind them around your neck, write them on the tablet of your heart. –Proverbs 3:3 NIV

WHEN I FIRST SET eyes on you, I didn't know what love was. I thought I did. At twenty-one, on my own for the first time, recovering from a broken engagement, I'd been disappointed in love too many times to chance it again. That first girls' night out was the beginning of a new stage in my life—playing the field. No way was I going to get involved in another relationship. I was flying high and free. And that's the way I wanted it to be.

Then you joined our table.

You stood out from the crowd—but it wasn't your six-foot-four-inch, lanky frame or bearded face or wavy hair that fell almost to your shoulders that drew me to you. It was your eyes—blue eyes that twinkled when you smiled. And you smiled a lot that night. You're the only one I remember dancing with. You and what's-his-name.

What's-his-name asked me out for Friday night. But the best part of that date—I was playing the field, remember?—was running into you. Suddenly a humdrum evening sparkled like those blue eyes of yours. The next evening we were out with the crowd again, and this time you and I were together. I felt safe with you.

Our first date was one week after my date with what's-his-name. You took me to see *Deliverance*. I hated it. But I loved being with you. After you took me home, we sat on the sofa in my second floor apartment eating White House ice cream. You fed me the cherries from yours.

"That's the man I'm going to marry," I announced to myself the next morning. So much for playing the field.

Over the next few weeks, we became an item, and my feelings for you grew so fast it scared me. So I broke up with you.

That was Friday night. By Sunday evening, I knew I'd made a big mistake. That was before the days of cell phones. I didn't even have your home number. I didn't even know where you lived, except way out of town in a village called Smithport.

I'd left the window shades up and the lights on all weekend—our signal that I was home—but you didn't stop by. You didn't call. So Sunday evening I went looking for you and found you at a restaurant not far out of town.

"I don't know how this will end up," I told you. "But however it does, I know I'd rather have you in my life than spend my days without you. This weekend was horrible."

After we were married, you told me it was a quirk you were in the restaurant. "It wasn't a place I usually went on Sunday evening."

That day was a turning point in my life. I decided to take a chance on love.

And I'm so glad I did.

Thank you, Lord, for the love of a lifetime. Amen.

MORE TEA: Read and meditate on 1 Corinthians 13.

What Is Love Made Of?

And now I will show you the most excellent way. –1 Corinthians 12:31b NIV

HUBBY AND I DON'T DO Valentine's Day. For some reason, it's never been an important event on our life calendar.

Oh, I tried to make it an event a few times. One year I cooked up a special dinner: roast beef heart and pink mashed potatoes, a meal we endured only once. A greeting card never seems to say what I want it to say, even when I make the card myself.

Perhaps it's that what I feel for my husband of forty-five years goes beyond words.

And I think the forty-five years has a lot to do with it.

In the early years, I looked for what I could get in the relationship: companionship, love, support, a listening ear, sympathy. What I got was a man who worked ten- to twelve-hour days five days a week, provided firewood, fixed things (an unending job because something always needs to be fixed), and built me a house. He's been a good father to our three children—a softy, I always called him. But his softness balanced my harshness.

I've never seen him angry—upset a few times, but never angry. Even when I tried to pick a fight, he never took the bait. And he's always supported me in my dreams. I dedicated my second book to him with these words: "To the man who fixes dinner, washes the dishes and clothes, dusts and vacuums, shops for groceries *and* puts them away, does the 'kid runs'— the myriad of daily tasks considered 'women's work'—so that I could have the time to write. To the man who told me that he felt God's will for his life was to free up my time so I could follow God's call for my life."

And whether I decided to go to work outside the home or quit the job I had, he's always supported my decisions.

Although he "suggests" ways my cooking could be improved, he's always eaten everything I've made, even when I couldn't.

And now that the nest is empty, he still looks for ways to help the kids out, being the handyman for our daughter in South Carolina when we visit, to our daughter-in-law next door when our son's job requires extended times away from home, and being the car repair guy and consultant when our youngest son's old car breaks down yet again. Whenever they call, any time of the day or night, he's available to them.

But we're learning to do things for us, too. We've set aside Friday night as our date night. No chores when he comes home from work—and he better be home by 5:30. Homemade pizza and a movie. But he rarely makes it through the movie. I hear his soft snores around nine. I don't even bother waking him up to go to bed. It never works and he doesn't even remember. I just cover him with a blanket, turn off the TV, turn down the lights, and softly kiss him on the forehead. He'll get to bed eventually.

I used to feel sorry for myself when he neglected to say "I love you" every day. But—don't tell him this—lately I've come to realize I don't need to hear it. I *see* it—in the tired lines around his eyes, in the gray streaks through his beard, in the increasing stoop of his shoulders, in the slower pace of his steps. I hear "I love you" shouted from the stack of firewood by the wood stove, from the packages of venison and vegetables and berries in the freezer, from the 1997 Explorer that he's fixed and fixed and fixed. The walls of the house he built are his arms around me day and night.

"Saturday's Valentine's Day," I said one night as we sat at the supper table.

He looked up. "What do you want to do?"

I smiled. "Nothing, really. I'm such a homebody anymore."

He smiled and nodded. He feels the same way. After a fifty-eight-hour week, all he wants is a good supper and a soft couch.

"We never did do Valentine's Day, did we?" I said. "I wonder why."

We ate in silence for a few minutes. Then it hit me.

"Because with you," I said, warmth coursing through me, "I have Valentine's Day every day."

Dear God, You gave me the perfect life companion. Not a perfect man, but the man perfect for me. Thank you. Amen.

MORE TEA: Read and meditate on 1 Corinthians 13.

Lent

Examine yourselves to see whether you are holding to your faith.

–2 Corinthians 13:5 NRSV

Forty Days

Examine yourselves, to see whether you are holding to your faith. Test yourselves. Do you not realize that Jesus Christ is in you? –2 Corinthians 13:5 RSV

EVER NOTICE HOW THE number forty occurs at critical moments in Scripture? It rained on the earth for forty days and forty nights. It was the number of days required to properly embalm a body for burial in ancient Egypt.

Moses, especially, is linked to the number. Not only did he lead the stubborn Israelites in the wilderness for forty years, but his life is divided into three forty-year periods: his Egyptian years, his shepherd years, and his wilderness years. He spent forty days and forty nights on Mount Sinai being personally tutored by God Himself in the law.

The Israelite spies cased the Promised Land for forty days. Goliath defied God for forty days. Elijah fasted in the desert for forty days. Jonah told the Ninevites they had forty days to get their act together before God would judge them.

Prior to beginning his earthly ministry, Jesus fasted and prayed in the wilderness for forty days and forty nights. And His final forty days on earth between His resurrection and ascension were spent giving last-minute instructions to His disciples.

Notice how the number is associated with judgment and preparation. Lent, the forty weekdays from Ash Wednesday to Easter Sunday commemorating Jesus' fasting in the wilderness, is a time of self-examination and spiritual preparation. We give up things, such as eating candy and pop or watching television, to practice self-denial and self-discipline.

But the most important part of this time should be examining our hearts, minds, and spirits, asking God to show us anything we harbor that hinders us in our spiritual growth.

First, examine your heart, the seat of our emotions and true character: Are your motives right? Do you choose love over hate, forgiveness over resentment, self-control over anger, contentment over envy, generosity over selfishness, faith over fear, humility over pride, hope over discouragement, trust over doubt, patience over impatience, thankfulness over complaining?

Next, examine your mind: Are you allowing God to transform and renew your mind? Or are you still hanging onto control of your thoughts, especially the bad ones? Are you capturing every thought and giving it to God? Are you filling your mind with the positive or the negative? Use Philippians 4:8 as your report card.

Now for the soul and spirit. According to the *Children's Ministry Resource Bible*, my soul is the part of me that responds to the world, while my spirit is the part of me that responds to God. I am not to love the world or the things of the world. Instead I am to fix my eyes on Jesus (Hebrews 12:2) and use Him as my model. Am I still running from Him, a rebel with my own agenda, and making myself miserable? Or am I running to Him, needing His love, forgiveness, strength, and wisdom as desperately as I need air? Do I allow Him to guide my footsteps, day by day, moment by moment, or do I insist that I do it my way?

Some pretty hard questions, but ones that God will help us with if only we ask.

Search me, O God, and know my heart. Try me, and know my thoughts; and see if there be any wicked way in me. And lead me in the way everlasting (Psalm 139:23–34). Amen.

MORE TEA: Read and meditate on Psalm 139.

Spring Cleaning

You are already made clean by the word that I have spoken to you. —
John 15:3 RSV

I DON'T SPRING CLEAN. My mother did, though. So did my mother-in-law. Both turned the house upside down every spring to get to the ceilings, walls, floors, and giving everything on and in them—and I mean *everything*—a good scrub-down.

It's not that I don't like a clean house. It's not that I'm lazy. It's just that I can't stand for things to be out of place. So I wait until I can't stand the dust anymore to get out my Swiffer duster. The floor I vacuum more often, now that I bought a new, lightweight upright that swivels and maneuvers around furniture like a sleek race car and is easier on my back. Occasionally I give the house a thorough cleaning, but not annually and not all at once. I can't handle that.

Just as I need to give my house a thorough cleaning periodically, so must I do the same with my spirit, going through room by room, tossing the trash and clutter that's accumulated, and sweeping away all the dust and dirt—the residue of everyday living.

My spiritual "Swiffer" is the Word of God; my vacuum cleaner, prayer. And what better time to do my spiritual spring cleaning than Lent? Beginning with Ash Wednesday and ending on Easter morning, Lent is a time to examine ourselves for anything that clutters and dirties our spirits, hindering our spiritual growth and thus our relationship with God.

That's why I'm taking a "40-Day Challenge" to read through the Gospels by Easter. Two chapters a day will get me through Matthew, Mark, Luke, and John. I can't think of a better way to prepare for Easter than to read through the accounts of the life and ministry of Christ written by His closest disciples.

I'm also keeping a SOAP journal, copying one verse of *Scripture* to meditate on ("S"); writing down in one or two sentences what I see (*observe*) in that verse ("O") and how to *apply* it to my life ("A"); and finally a one- or two-sentence *prayer* ("P") relating to the verse. I like the SOAP format because wordy me has to be concise, and it's in that very conciseness that the meaning shines like a cleaned and polished room.

Prayer is also a vital aspect of the 40-Day Challenge. Prayer is simply talking to God. I keep a prayer journal at the back of my SOAP journal. I note personal prayers and requests for others. I pray for needs on my heart, folks and situations the Holy Spirit brings to mind as I pray. I also record when and how my prayers are answered.

My spiritual spring cleaning may turn things topsy-turvy. Although I like order and organization, I've got to give God room to work—and trust Him for the results.

Why not take the 40-Day Challenge with me?

Create in me a clean heart, O God, and renew a new and right spirit within me. Search me and know my heart. Try me, and know my thoughts; and see if there be any wicked way in me, and lead me in the way everlasting. Amen. (Based on Psalms 51:10 and 139:23, 24)

MORE TEA: Read and meditate on Psalm 19:7–14.

MORE TEA for the 40-Day Challenge: 2 Timothy 3:16; Jeremiah 29:13; James 4:8; Psalms 51 and 139; Hebrews 4:12.

The Subtle Sins

Create in me a pure heart, O God, and renew a steadfast spirit within me. –Psalm 51:10 NIV

I'M ASHAMED TO ADMIT it, but I haven't dusted my house since before Christmas. Call it laziness, call it setting priorities, call it avoidance, call it denial ("It's not that bad"), call it whatever you want. But it's such a futile activity, especially in the winter. Especially if you have a woodburner. Especially if your furnace has a blower. I could dust one day, and the next it doesn't even look like it.

The only time the thickening accumulation bothers me is when the sun is shining. But I haven't seen the sun very much lately. Only gray, dreary skies and snow flying sideways. But eventually the sun will return, and the dust shall be dealt with. (No cracks about Genesis 3:19, please: "For dust you are, and to dust you shall return.")

Just as the dust accumulates in my house if I don't deal with it, so sin accumulates in my heart. Call it laziness, call it setting priorities, call it avoidance, call it denial, call it what you will, but if not dealt with, it results in spiritual dryness, an empty prayer life, and stunted Christian growth.

Lent has always been a time for spiritual introspection, a time to clean my spiritual house and get rid of the hindrances, time to face the ugly things I'd rather keep hidden, for I'm ashamed they even exist in me.

Yet I'm an imperfect human being, struggling to live a godly life in an ungodly world. I don't lie (outright), but is there any way I deceive others? I haven't murdered anyone, but have I, by spreading gossip, murdered someone's reputation? I claim to love others, but do I harbor bitterness or envy or unforgiveness in my heart?

A couple of months ago, I discussed unanswered prayer with a friend at church. I couldn't understand why there seemed to be a roadblock to book publishing. My first novel was considered by the publishing committee at several houses only to be turned down again and again. In addition, speaking and teaching gigs had dried up.

He asked if there was unconfessed sin in my life. I told him I'd considered it, but didn't really see anything. I prayed for God to show me, but He knew I wasn't ready. I really didn't want to see, didn't want to know. God always brings us to a place of readiness first.

Then we started a two-week prayer and fasting time for a writers and speakers network I belong to. Many needed breakthroughs, especially financial. The first devotional was about sin hindering prayer. Once again I prayed, "Lord, show me . . ."

And He did. The sin was envy. Not a strong presence (so I thought), but a grasping one. I don't want to say "little," because no sin is little in the eyes of God. But when others would ask for prayer for favor for their book proposals, for book contracts or speaking engagements, the envy would stir. "I want that for me, too!" I'd cry silently. And I wouldn't—I couldn't—pray with a sincere heart. *If you couldn't have it, why should they?* Envy whispered.

For so long I either denied the envy I harbored or refused to acknowledge it was big and strong enough to affect me and make a difference. I was wrong.

Unlike dusting my house, cleaning the accumulated dirt in my heart is not futile. It's vital.

Lord, pluck this envy out of my heart! Then spray the weed killer of Your Word to destroy any root left behind. Plant the seed of Your love to grow and spread and blossom and give off a sweet fragrance. Envy has hidden in me for a long time, and I will have to be on my guard, watching for it in case it sprouts again. Never again will I underestimate the cost and the power of this deadly sin. Only through the blood of Your Son, Jesus, can I overcome this and live the life You have called me to live. I thank You for Your patience, steadfast love, and unending mercy and grace. In the name of Him who died so that I might live, Jesus Christ, my Savior and Lord of my life. Amen.

MORE TEA: Read and meditate on James 3:13–4:10.

"I" Trouble

Do not think of yourself more highly than you ought. –Romans 12:3 NIV

"I CAN SEE!" I emailed several friends. "No more lugging around a magnifying glass from room to room."

I hadn't realized how bad my eyes had gotten since my eye doctor appointment a year earlier. I should have recognized the symptoms—I'd been down this road before. First I complain the letters on everything from ibuprofen bottles to coupons to nutrition labels are too small. "How do they expect people to read such tiny letters?" I grumble. Over time, I gradually realize the problem is not with "them," but with me.

But still I was amazed when I got my new eyeglasses how clearer the letters were in my daily devotional booklet, on my computer screen, and even my own handwriting. Ever try to write with a pen in one hand and a magnifying glass in the other? I don't know how many emails I sent with misspellings and typos because I couldn't see. I honestly hadn't realized how bad my eyes really were.

Now I know.

I'm the same way with sin. First I deny I have a problem. I haven't murdered anyone or cheated on my income taxes. One time I even went back into the grocery store when I realized the checkout person didn't charge me for a package of lunch meat. I was pretty proud of myself that day. Almost broke my arm patting myself on the back.

But sin is subtle, sneaky. Like the envy I thought I didn't have until God revealed it to me. Like the pride He's shown me this week.

"I can't be proud, Lord," I protest.

I remind Him of how I've stopped fishing for compliments and how well I've learned to keep my mouth shut or add "Lord willing" or "praise God" to anything that sounds like I might be boasting. I jog His memory (like it needs jogging) about how I do things for others more and expect them to do things for me less.

"Look how far I've come, Lord," I say once I've bored Him with my goody-two-shoes list.

But look how far you have to go.

And then it's His turn to remind me—of the times I say, "Don't those idiots know they're supposed to turn on their headlights when it's snowing/raining/foggy?" Or when I complain about drivers who don't use turn signals, abuse the right-turn-on-red law, run red lights, don't come to a complete stop at stop signs, don't stop for pedestrians waiting to cross the street (especially if I'm the pedestrian), or blast me with their high beams. It's like I'm a good Christian everywhere but behind the wheel.

Lurking in me is a critical spirit that shows itself when I judge others. They might be wrong, but, like the Good Book says, I've got to take the log out of my own eye first.

There's a fine line, I've learned, between pride and humility. Not a gulf, not a chasm, as we so often think. But a sneaky, subtle, sometimes invisible line only the magnifying glass of God's Word and the updated eyeglasses of His Holy Spirit can reveal.

Not all pride is sinful. It's okay to have pride of country, of accomplishment, or family—note national pride during the Olympics. It's okay to break out the pictures of your kids and grandkids, to plaster a cling-on to your vehicle displaying the name of your little All-Star.

My mother never bragged about me. Maybe that's why I have such a problem with pride. With being tempted to think of myself more highly than I ought. With denying that I have a problem with pride.

Where does pride cross the line from being honorable to sinful?

When pride focuses on self and becomes self-serving and blossoms into conceit, egotism, judgmentalism, and selfish ambition. It's eye-opening to look up the synonyms of these words.

But, when we're ready, God works in and with us to pluck out the root of pride so we won't have so much "I" trouble.

Search me, O God, and know my heart; test my thoughts. Point out anything You find in me that makes You sad, and lead me along the path of everlasting life. Create in me a new, clean heart, filled with clean thoughts and right desires. Amen. (From Psalms 139:23–24; 51:10 LB)

MORE TEA: Read and meditate on Matthew 7:1–5.

"I" Trouble

perception
fuzzy
can't see too far ahead
headaches
from "I" strain
use my "I's" too much
without
the right light

need to
give my "I's" a rest
see the world
through the lens
of selflessness
and
in the light of
God's Word.

Piece of Mind or Peace of Mind?

Be transformed by the renewing of your mind. –Romans 12:2 NIV

IT HAD BEEN A long week. I was learning a new job at work, driving all over western Pennsylvania shopping for a car for my daughter—and suffering sticker shock in the process—hanging out laundry after dark, and trying to keep my cool.

The flat tire fifty miles from home didn't help much, but I was proud of the way I handled myself after Mr. Road Rage tailgated me for several miles, then gave me a not-too-friendly wave as he roared past. Could it have been that I was just too tired to respond? Or was it that I was still thinking about the man who saw me and my daughter struggling with the jack and stopped on his way home from work and changed the tire for us?

Although this incident happened many years ago, I never forgot it, nor the life lesson it hammered home: I really am what I think (Proverbs 23:7). My thoughts have a powerful effect on what I do and say, on my attitude about anything. Dwelling on the obstacles I face, the mistakes I make, and the unkind things people do only makes me frustrated, stressed, and angry. But thinking about the good things that happen, however small, helps me to get through the tough times and become a better person.

Sins of the mind are subtle and sneaky because of their very privacy. No one knows what I'm thinking unless I reveal it. So I can think all the thoughts I want, no matter how bad they are, right? Wrong!

Sins of the mind are like a slow-growing tumor that masks its presence behind easily explained symptoms—until it becomes so big and exerts such devastating effects it can no longer be ignored. It must be dealt with, and swiftly. But by then, the damage is often irreversible.

What are the sins of the mind? Harboring unhealthy thoughts, whether they be about the ways people have hurt us and the revenge we could seek, fantasies that have no substance in real life but give us momentary pleasure, addictions, a "poor-me" mentality that dwells on how everything seems to go wrong for me and right for someone else, another person's faults . . . the list goes on—you fill in the blanks.

There's no such thing as the thought police who bang on the door of my mind and arrest my unhealthy thoughts. I am the only one who controls what I think. It is I who must capture every thought and rein it in (2 Corinthians 10:5). That's why sins of the mind are so dangerous. It's like the fox guarding the henhouse. I need help!

When I want to rinse out a glass of water into which one of those pesky ladybug-like insects falls, I often hold it under running water, letting the clean water displace the contaminated water. This principle of displacement works for cleaning out unhealthy thoughts from the mind, too. Replacing the bad thoughts that contaminate my spirit, behavior, relationships, and reputation with good thoughts doesn't happen overnight. It's a process.

Getting rid of the bad thoughts by filling my mind with the Word of God is like placing that dirty water glass under a wellspring of clean, fresh, renewing water (Hebrews 4:12). "Whatever is true, whatever is noble, whatever is right, whatever is pure, whatever is lovely, whatever is admirable—if anything is excellent or praiseworthy—think about such things," Paul wrote. "And the peace of God will be with you" (Philippians 4:8).

I have a choice—*piece* of mind or *peace* of mind. Piece of mind leads to turmoil. Peace of mind leads to harmony and serenity. Funny how it all comes down to one letter—the letter "I."

Examine me, God, and know my mind; test me, and discover my thoughts. Find out if there is any deceit in me, and guide me in the eternal way. Amen. (Psalm 139:23–24 TEV)

MORE TEA: Read and meditate on Philippians 4:8.

A Heart Like His

Each of you should look not only to your own interests, but also to the interests of others. –Philippians 2:4 NIV

FOR TWO WEEKS I was able to read without a magnifying glass. Then a tiny speck appeared on the edge of the right lens of my new eyeglasses. At first I thought it was an ink spot. But cleaning the lens didn't remove it. *Maybe it won't get any bigger.* I dreaded the thought of having to send them back. It had been wonderful, being able to see my computer screen and the printed page clearly. But a few days later, the speck expanded and resembled a chip on a windshield. In addition, a minuscule crack had appeared in the left lens.

So back to the eye doctor I went. And learned that our insurance requires them to use the company that manufactured the lenses.

"They do shoddy work," the doctor's assistant told me. The lenses were made too big, and the pressure of being forced into frames too small had caused them to crack.

"How long will it take—another seven to ten days?" I asked. "Maybe since this is a return due to their mistake, they'll speed up the process?"

She shook her head. "It doesn't matter. They don't care. They have so much business that one customer doesn't make a difference."

Putting the customer first, quality products, and quality service have taken a backseat to me, myself, and I—and big customers with deep pockets. Corporate hearts have hardened toward the little guy.

But before I call the kettle black, perhaps I should look into my own heart. Where have I become callous?

Have I attended to the physical needs of others or do I just wish them well (James 2:14–16)? Do I give generously (Ephesians 4:28) or am I tightfisted with my money, possessions, time, and talents (2 Corinthians 9:6–11)? I think of Haiti, people in Third World countries, Russian children who live in sewers, and I feel overwhelmed by the quantity and depth of the needs. I think of the many organizations that respond to these needs, and I allow confusion over which organization to give to hold me back from giving as I should.

God wants us to have a heart like His. He commanded us to show mercy and compassion to one another (Zechariah 7:9), to act justly and to love mercy (Micah 6:8), to clothe ourselves with tenderhearted mercy (Colossians 3:12). Having no interest in or concern for other people, their needs, and activities is indifference, another of the subtle sins God has brought to my attention.

When I was a little girl, I used to lie in bed at night, dreaming of going to Third World countries to help others. My desire to make a difference was so strong, I couldn't get to sleep. My heart would break when I'd see the aged, the blind, the crippled, the infirm, the helpless. I wanted to do something. I even looked into the Peace Corps when I was in college.

But somewhere along the way, I lost that passion to help others. My life, by my own choices, took a different direction. Then God used my flippant response to a local tragedy to show me how far I've gotten from that tenderhearted young girl and the places in my heart that have become hard, calloused. I'm too often like the priest and the Levite in Jesus' story of the Good Samaritan, who either didn't want to take the time or get their hands dirty helping someone else.

Just like the speck in my eyeglass lens grew bigger and bigger until I had to send them back to the maker, so the sin of indifference has grown to a defect in my character. In order to correct the flaw and for my heart to become a heart like God's—tender, compassionate, loving—it, too, must be sent back to the Maker, who promised, "I will give you a new heart and put a new spirit in you; I will remove from you your heart of stone and give you a heart of flesh" (Ezekiel 36:26 NIV).

Create in me a clean heart, O God, and put a new and right spirit within me (Psalm 51:10 RSV). Amen.

MORE TEA: Read and meditate on Luke 10:30–37; Isaiah 58:6–9.

Spring Thaw

See! The winter is past; the rains are over and gone. Flowers appear on the earth; the season of singing has come. —Song of Songs 2:11–12 NIV

IN 1871 HORATIO GATES SPAFFORD, a well-known American lawyer and church elder, lost everything he had in the Great Chicago Fire. Two years later an iron sailing vessel struck the steamship *Ville du Havre*, which carried Spafford's family, and it sank. Spafford's daughters, ages eleven, nine, five, and two, were among the 256 people who perished. He immediately set out for England to join his wife, who survived the disaster. It was on that voyage, at the very site the *Ville du Havre* went down, Spafford penned the words of the well-known hymn "It Is Well with My Soul." Seven years later, his only son died of scarlet fever at the age of four.

A fire that destroyed all he owned. A shipwreck that claimed the lives of his children. An epidemic that took the life of his only son. Sure sounds like a nineteenth-century Job. Yet Spafford, like Job, refused to let these tragedies diminish his faith in a God that promised never to leave or forsake him. He may have questioned God about the tragedies, but he blamed neither God nor others. He knew blame only led to bitterness, another of the subtle sins. He knew a bitter spirit poisons itself and spews that poison on everyone with ears to hear. So he allowed these seasons of trial to make him better.

A year and a half later Spafford, his wife, and two daughters (born to them after the shipwreck) headed to Jerusalem to minister to the people there, regardless of their religion, without trying to convert them. In doing so, he established what later became known as the "American Colony." It was here in 1881 that Spafford died from malaria and was buried.

Trials are often called "the winter of the soul."

In the winter, the ground freezes. The harsher and colder the winter, the deeper the frost level. In the spring, the earth leans more and more toward the sun, the temperatures warm up, the sun shines longer each day, and warmer winds begin to blow. The frozen earth begins to thaw. At first the ground is muddy and mushy, but still unyielding in places. Water, like tears, seeps from the earth and shows where the frost is coming out of the ground. Eventually the frost leaves the ground completely, the sun and the wind combine to dry up the mud and mess, crocuses and daffodils pop up, and the grass turns green again.

We've all endured at least one winter of the soul, a prolonged period of time that can cause our spirits to grow cold and to harden. No one, not even the strongest Christian you know, not even those who have dedicated their lives to serving God, is immune from the heartbreaks of life. Indeed, these are the very times that will make or break our faith.

Winter, though, is only a season. When we, like the earth, lean more toward the Son and submit our hearts to the wind of the Holy Spirit, the frost of bitterness seeps out of our spirits, and we, too, can sing, even with tears, "It is well with my soul."

When peace like a river attendeth my way, when sorrows like sea billows roll, whatever my lot, thou hast taught me to say, It is well, it is well with my soul. Thank you, Lord. Amen.*

*From "It Is Well with My Soul," words by Horatio G. Spafford. Public domain.

MORE TEA: Read and meditate on Job 1:13–2:10.

Follow Through

People who promise things that they never give are like clouds and wind that bring no rain. –Proverbs 25:14 GNT

WHEN I WAS IN high school, my father took up golf. He wasn't an avid golfer, though—just took up the sport to calm his jangled nerves. Daddy's girl that I was, I signed up for golfing lessons the school offered. Between my father and the golf instructor, I learned two things were vital to success: correct form and follow-through.

"Follow through" means "to carry something through to its completion." In sports, to follow through means to complete the swing or motion after the ball has been hit or released.

Why is following through important, when the ball is no longer in your control? I don't understand the physics of it, but I do understand that if you don't follow through, the ball won't go where you want it to. When my son was a baseball pitcher, for instance, he would neglect to follow through on his pitching motion when he was tired. The result was that he didn't hit his spots—or, in lay language, the ball didn't go where he wanted it to go. The same principle applies to swinging a golf club or a baseball bat. The follow through is crucial to a solid hit.

Following through isn't important only in sports. It's important in life itself.

Ever have someone promise you something and not give you what was promised? I'm not just talking businesses, manufacturers, or salespersons here. Or have someone borrow something and fail to return it by the time he said he would? Or give you a time to meet you and show up late—or not show up at all? It's no fun being on the wrong end of a false promise. It breaks trust, poisons relationships, and ruins character.

But what if you're the one who's given your word?

"Promise me something," someone urges you.

"Okay," you say without thinking, when the correct response should have been, "What do you want me to promise?"

Sometimes we make false promises because we want to look good or we don't want to disappoint others. I've often made pledges to organizations (mostly those that phone me with their spiel), then never followed through. Most of the time I wanted to give what I promised, but when the time came, the money was needed elsewhere. Eventually I learned to ask them to mail me the material and I would consider it. People-pleasers like me have difficulty saying no. I actually convinced myself I would make good on my pledge.

Sometimes we make false promises to get someone off our backs—like our spouse or our kids, who know what buttons to push when they want something. Sometimes, like Peter in today's reading, we really mean it in the heat of the moment, but then reality sets in and we balk. Or we accept an invitation and then call with excuses when something better comes up—or even, worse, we don't call at all.

Or we vow to forsake all others, and to love and cherish, for better or worse, in sickness and in health, till death do us part, and then break that vow.

Jesus said we will give account for every idle, or careless, word we utter (Matthew 12:36–37).

Not following through on our word not only casts a shadow on our reputation, character, and integrity, but it also hurts others, especially those closest to us—those we really don't want to hurt. Perhaps we gave our word, whether or not we meant it at the time, because we didn't want to hurt someone.

But which is worse? Believing a lie told by someone you trust or hearing the truth spoken in love? Which is harder to deal with—sincerity or insincerity?

My parents taught me to follow through on my promises, no matter the cost. The cost of not following through, though, is far greater. I want to be known as a person who keeps her word. I want people to trust me and believe me. It has to do with those old-fashioned things like principle and honor and integrity.

On the links of life, always remember to follow through—it's the only way to put power in your swing.

May the words of my mouth and the meditation of my heart be pleasing in your sight, O LORD, my Rock and my Redeemer (Psalm 141:3). Amen.

MORE TEA: Read and meditate on Matthew 26:31–35.

Fillers

Keep away from anything that might take God's place in your hearts. –1 John 5:21 NLT

I'VE LONG BEEN A health nut. My kids call me "Dr. Mom" and still summon me when health issues arise in their lives (or their kids' lives). When they were little, I bought *The American Medical Association Family Medical Guide* and kept it under my side of the bed. When anyone got sick, I'd check the symptoms with the medical guide. Even when they weren't sick, I'd pull the heavy volume out and pore through its pages.

These days I browse the internet. With countless websites pertaining to health, it's important to glean information only from trustworthy sites and to compare data. I trust the sites that aren't trying to sell me something, that are there simply to educate and inform.

That's why I subscribe to *Consumer Reports* and its corresponding health newsletter. *CR* doesn't sell advertising so it can be completely objective. Products and services reported on have been tested thoroughly and objectively. With my first issue came *Consumer Reports The Best of Health: 280 Questions you've always wanted to ask your doctor.*

Since I've long dealt with unrelenting symptoms of hypothyroidism, I flipped to the thyroid section. I'd already known that broccoli and triclosan, an ingredient in antibacterial soap, interfered with the thyroid. I'd checked the labels of all the soap products in the house, replaced dish detergent and hand soap, and bought a packet of antibacterial hand wipes that didn't contain triclosan to keep in my purse. You don't know what's in those hand soap dispensers in public restrooms.

My eyebrows raised when I read that soy may interfere with the absorption of synthroid, the medicine I take daily for low thyroid. Soy—and anything containing soy—can be consumed, but not until at least eight hours after taking the medicine. Once again I began reading labels—and was surprised by what all contained soy. My coffee creamer and my "healthy" cereal both contain soy. So does my multivitamin powder that's supposed to have been formulated to boost thyroid function!

"It's used as a filler," my husband said when I told him. And here I'd thought soy was supposed to be good for you.

So I'm back to reading labels again. I'll do anything to be healthy and feel well.

But do I have the same attitude when it comes to my spiritual health? Am I as careful with what I consume with my eyes and my ears as what I do with my mouth? I wouldn't think of skipping a meal, yet how often do I forgo a quiet time, when I read the Bible, meditate, and pray? What fillers have snuck into my life that, although they appeared to be good for me at first, really interfere with my relationship with God? God doesn't just *want* to be first in my life—He *commands* it: "I am the LORD your

God. . . . You must not have any other god but me" (Exodus 20:2, 3).

It's too easy to let the fillers sneak in. Fillers are just that—they take up space but add no nutritional value.

I need to be a spiritual health nut, too.

As I examine my heart, soul, mind, and life this Lenten season, Lord, show me the fillers that threaten to take Your place. Amen.

MORE TEA: Read and meditate on Exodus 20:1–11.

From Amazed to Afraid

Now they were on the road, going up to Jerusalem, and Jesus was going before them; and they were amazed. And as they followed, they were afraid. –Mark 10:32 NKJV

JESUS WAS WALKING INTO a lion's den. The disciples knew the Pharisees were just waiting for a chance to get rid of Him. They'd witnessed the many times the Pharisees had tried to trap Jesus. And they'd heard the words of warning Jesus had given them twice before: that He would suffer terrible things when He went to Jerusalem, be rejected by the religious powers that be, and be killed. And He'd rise from the dead.

They knew danger lay ahead, but there was no convincing Jesus to stay out of Jerusalem. They couldn't fathom it. Their sense was to protect their Master, to keep Him with them as long as possible. Why would He knowingly go to a place where death awaited Him? They were amazed not only that He dared to go but also that His steps were firm, His attitude resolute.

Amazement was nothing new to the disciples. It had been a daily occurrence for the three years they'd followed Him, lived with Him, learned from Him. But their amazement turned to fear as they drew nearer to the "City of Peace." Did Jesus *want* to die?

Yes. He had to, for only the sinless Lamb could become the sacrifice needed to take away our sins. This wasn't what they signed on for three years earlier when Jesus invited them to follow Him. They thought He'd set up His kingdom and they'd be the bigwigs. James and John even asked to sit on either side of Him—the places of highest honor. How little they understood!

Isn't it the same with us? When we first decide to follow Jesus, we're excited, amazed, hopeful for what's ahead. Then things don't turn out the way we expect. Instead of reward for our sacrifices, for our good deeds, we get trials and troubles. Like the disciples, we don't fathom the eternal significance of our decision or of our daily choices. We don't want to wait for our rewards. We want to enjoy them now. We follow Him in amazement at first, then as the road gets steeper and we begin to understand the real cost of following Jesus, the fear sets in.

The remedy for fear is to do what Jesus did: focus on the Father. Like Corrie ten Boom said: "Never be afraid to trust the unknown future to a known God."

Never let the amazement of following You dwindle, O Lord. Keep my face set to Jerusalem. Amen.

MORE TEA: Read and meditate on Mark 10:32–34.

Holy Week

For God so loved the world that He gave His only begotten Son, that whoever believes in Him should not perish but have everlasting life.

–John 3:16 NKJV

Cross or Chorus?

Purify my motives, Lord.
Replace myself with Thyself.

Ah, can You do this painlessly?
So I don't have to grieve
the death of self.

Replace the cross with a chorus,
so I can sing, not weep;
rejoice, nor mourn;
feel wholeness, not brokenness.

Or
perhaps the cross and the chorus
go together.

For
without the cross
there'd be no chorus.

For our light affliction, which is but for a moment,
is working for us a far more exceeding
and eternal weight of glory.
–2 Corinthians 4:17

An Unexpected Answer

"For my thoughts are not your thoughts, neither are your ways my ways," declares the LORD. –Isaiah 55:8 NIV

I QUIT TEACHING WHEN my first child was born, believing that being home was more important than the extra income. Deep down, I hoped someday I'd return to the profession I loved and that God would reward me for sacrificing my career for my family. A year before the youngest was to start kindergarten, I told God I'd do anything He wanted me to do. I envisioned teaching again or perhaps having a music ministry. Three months later I discovered I was pregnant.

"God!" I cried, shaking my fist at the ceiling. "How could You do this to me? This was not was I had in mind!"

It took me five years to get over my shock and anger. I realize now how selfishness had limited my perspective. The child God blessed us with *was* the answer to my prayer. But you couldn't tell me that then.

The crowds that waved palm branches and laid their robes on the ground in front of Jesus as He rode a donkey colt into

Jerusalem that first Palm Sunday were expecting something different, too. They were hoping this prophet from Nazareth was the promised Messiah that would free them from Rome's oppression. That this miracle worker would keep them in food and good health. So they welcomed him with cries of "Hosanna!" By the end of the week, though, they were shouting, "Crucify Him!"

Why the change of heart? Because instead of overthrowing the Roman governor and zapping his soldiers, He condemned their own religious leaders and threw the vendors out of the temple. He preached peace, not rebellion; forgiveness, not retribution. They wanted relief from Roman rule and good things on earth. Instead they got a Savior from their sin and the promise of eternal life with God.

"I have come that they might have life," Jesus said, "and have it to the full."

Some still don't get it today. Do you?

Forgive me, God, for my temper tantrums when I don't get my way. Remind me that Your way is always the best way. Amen.

MORE TEA: Read and meditate on Matthew 21:1–9.

The Greatest

Whoever wants to become great among you must be your servant. –
Matthew 20:26 NIV

I'LL NEVER FORGET THE time during my first year of teaching when I introduced my class to the school's "maintenance engineer." I thought a fancy title would make him sound more important. But Stoney would have none of it.

"Honey," he boomed in a voice that echoed down the hall, "I'm the janitor!"

He had one arm—the other had been amputated above the elbow—but that didn't stop him from doing what needed to be done. He cleaned the building, fixed what needed to be repaired, built bookshelves for my classroom, and tamed my youthful exuberance with his fatherly wisdom. Over forty years later, that janitor is still on the top of my "People I Admire" list.

But not everyone is like Stoney. A young man I once met told me he wanted political power, and all the wealth and prestige that goes with it. I felt sorry for him. You could be top dog one day and in the doghouse the next. He didn't understand that greatness doesn't come from an elevated position—it comes from a servant heart.

That was something the self-serving Pharisees of Jesus' day didn't understand, either. Considering themselves above the law, they manufactured ways to avoid doing what God wanted them to do while making things hard for the little guy. They took the best seats in church and at dinners, did good only to hear praise, dressed to the nines, loved titles, and prided themselves on keeping the letter of the law, even though they'd long lost the spirit of it. Instead of seeing Jesus' miracles, instead of seeing hurting people helped, they complained that Jesus was breaking their man-made laws.

Things really haven't changed much. It seems everyone wants to be number one. But Jesus showed us the only way to become great is by serving one another.

Remind me, Lord, that popularity and power are fleeting. Give me a servant's heart so I can live a life that is pleasing to You. Amen.

MORE TEA: Read and meditate on Matthew 23:1–36.

Waiting for the Answers

"I am the resurrection and the life. He who believes in me will live, even though he dies; and whoever lives and believes in me will never die. Do you believe this?" –Jesus, first century A.D., as quoted in John 11:25 NIV

LAZARUS WAS DYING. So his sisters, Martha and Mary, sent messengers to their friend Jesus, who had healed many. Surely He would come, and quickly. But Lazarus died shortly after the messengers left, and the grieving sisters buried him, grief mingling with hope. Hadn't He raised Jairus' daughter and the widow's son? But He must come soon, for both had been raised the same day they died.

The messengers returned after two days. Surely Jesus was right behind them. Another day passed, and no word from Jesus. Hope dwindled. Where was He? Didn't He care? Was He hurt? Sick? Perhaps the Pharisees had finally gotten their hands on Him. By the fourth day, Lazarus' body had begun to decompose. Then someone reported Jesus was on the Bethany road. Martha rushed out to meet Him.

"Lord, if You had been here, my brother would not have died." Was there accusation in her voice?

Hope, though, was not dead, like the cold, hard corpse in the tomb. "But even now, I believe that God will give whatever You ask."

What a statement of faith! But she faltered when Jesus told her Lazarus would rise again.

"Oh, I know he'll rise on the last day, on resurrection day, when everyone else rises," she said.

Jesus shook His head.

"I am the resurrection and the life," He said. "He who believes in me will live, even though he dies; and whoever lives and believes in me will never die."

Then the challenge: "Do you believe this?"

We know the rest of the story: how Martha confessed Him as the Messiah, the Son of God, but when Jesus commanded the stone be moved from the tomb's entrance, protested, "but he's been dead *four days!* The body's begun to stink!"

How much like Martha I am! I profess faith in Jesus, yet hedge when He challenges me to a higher and deeper level of that faith. I call to Him in trouble and wait for Him to answer, first patiently, then, when it seems no answer is forthcoming, wonder where He is when I'm hurting, why He hasn't answered. After all, hadn't I professed faith in Him and served Him faithfully?

Don't we all question God when life is beating us up? A writing colleague fighting a fierce battle with cancer recently wrote, "Faith is living without the answers."

Maybe all I need to know are the two truths Jesus stated when He told Martha He is the resurrection and the life: The believer's body may die, but will be resurrected when Jesus returns. Second, and even more important, the believer's soul will never die, for, once we receive eternal life through faith in Him, we will never be separated from the source of that life, Jesus.

Lord, I'm not a patient person. I want answers to my prayers either now or soon. Remind me that true faith is living without the answers and knowing, for the believer, every day is resurrection day. Amen.

MORE TEA: Read and meditate on 1 Kings 19; John 11:1–37.

A Faithful Friend

Carry each other's burdens. —Galatians 6:2 NIV

I DON'T KNOW WHAT I'd do without my friend Sharon. We met at a Bible study more than forty years ago and discovered we had much in common. We were both stay-at-home mothers struggling with more month than money, hard-working husbands, and unfulfilled dreams.

As our friendship grew, I'd find myself dialing her number whenever I needed someone to talk to, cheer me up, or give me advice. We spent hours analyzing life, the world, our children, and our men. I could tell her things I couldn't even tell my husband and knew she'd understand.

No matter how busy she was, no matter what time of the day I called, she took the time to listen, talk, and, most important, pray with me. Even when I didn't ask, I knew I could count on her prayers.

As our children grew, our lives became more complicated and the calls less frequent. But even though we're both busy, I know I can call her when a crisis arises.

On the night before He died, Jesus took Peter, James, and John with Him to the Garden of Gethsemane.

"My soul is overwhelmed with sorrow to the point of death," He told them. "Stay here and keep watch with Me."

But the busy day, big meal, and evening of fellowship took their toll. They fell asleep, waking only when Judas returned with a club-carrying, sword-wielding crowd. When Jesus needed them most, they let Him down. Perhaps if they had prayed instead of slept, they would not have deserted Him, leaving Him to suffer and die alone.

There are times when people ask us to pray for them. Are we like the sleepy trio whose spirit was willing and flesh was weak? Or are we like my friend Sharon, whose faithfulness and prayers make all the difference?

Thank You, Lord, for a friend who prays with and for me when I face my own Gethsemanes. May I be as faithful a friend to others as she is to me. Amen.

MORE TEA: Read and meditate on Matthew 26:36–46.

Betrayed

He who conceals his sins does not prosper, but whoever confesses and renounces them finds mercy. –Proverbs 28:13 NIV

SHE SAT SQUIRMING.

To what do I owe this visit? I wondered. I hadn't seen Tammy for nearly a year. Neither of us had kept up the friendship that grew when we first met on campus during my sophomore year in college. It was now summer, and I was taking my last class before graduating. In another month I'd be moving on.

"I've come to ask your forgiveness," she began.

Forgiveness? What for?

"Do you remember last fall when you were in the lobby with Jason, waiting for me to let you know when Penny got back?"

We'd planned a surprise birthday party for one of the girls on our floor. Since she was out and we didn't know when she'd be back, I thought I'd squeeze in some time with my boyfriend. Tammy, who had agreed to come get me when she returned, had come to the lobby and told me that Penny still wasn't back, but she'd let me know as soon as she showed up.

"I lied," she said now.

"What do you mean?"

"When I told you Penny wasn't back. She was. After I left you, I went back and told the girls that you didn't want to come up. That you'd rather spend the time with Jason."

I was floored. *So that's why I don't have any friends anymore.*

Jesus knew what it was like to be betrayed by a close friend, too. Judas Iscariot went down in history as a traitor. Almost immediately after Jesus' arrest, he was sorry and threw the money he received back into the temple, then went out and committed suicide. Perhaps he felt his sin was too great to be forgiven. Perhaps he thought it was too late.

Tammy felt remorse for what she did and asked for forgiveness and a relationship was healed. Judas didn't.

Thank You , Lord, that no matter what we've done, You will forgive us—if only we ask. Amen.

MORE TEA: Read and meditate on Matthew 26:14–16; 27:3–5.

Broken Promises

The sacrifice acceptable to God is a broken spirit; a broken and contrite heart, O God, you will not despise. –Psalm 51:17 NIV

MIKE WAS THE FIRST real boyfriend I had in high school. I went with him for three whole months during the spring of my sophomore year, when love blooms like the flowers. Then, on the bus after our class picnic in June, he gave me a note.

"Don't read this now," he whispered. "But when you do, remember that I'll always love you no matter what."

Dummy me believed him. Even after I read the "Dear Michele" letter. Even when I heard through the grapevine that he was chasing a cheerleader he had his eye on.

It would have been much easier if he had just told the truth in the first place—that he was ditching me for another girl. But instead, he told me a lie that gave me false hope. It wasn't until school started again that I woke up and smelled the roses—and they were rotten.

Broken promises. Broken hearts. Peter, too, made a promise he didn't keep. He told Jesus that he would never desert Him, even if he had to die with Him. A few hours later, Peter denied three times he even knew Jesus, cursing and swearing to emphasize his point.

All it took was one look from Jesus, and remorse flooded his soul. He went out of the courtyard where he'd been waiting and wept bitterly. He was a broken man. The next time we read of Peter, though, he's racing to the empty tomb.

Peter had finally met himself face-to-face. He saw his weakness and knew he was helpless to change. But when he took his brokenness to God, he was forgiven and made over. Peter never deserted his Lord again.

That's what God can do for us, if we let Him. But we have to be broken first. Then God can make us over into what He had planned for us to be all along.

Only through You, O God, can brokenness turn into wholeness. Thank You for making me over, better than I was before. Amen.

MORE TEA: Read and meditate on Luke 22:31–34, 55–62.

When Fair Is Foul

Wanting to satisfy the crowd, Pilate released Barabbas to them. He had Jesus flogged, and handed him over to be crucified. –Mark 15:15 NIV

THE GUIDANCE COUNSELOR STOOD at the classroom door, holding a sheet of paper. It was a list of students the substitute teacher had caught cheating on an assignment.

"Think of what you're doing," the counselor told her.

He scanned the list, pointing to several names.

"There's going to be a huge scandal when this gets out. These are good kids. Some of them are school board members' children."

He glanced up from the list, concern in his eyes.

"You want a job here, don't you?"

The implication was clear: turn your head and overlook the wrong, or forget ever having a permanent job in that district.

"But cheating is wrong," the teacher insisted. "I can't pretend it didn't happen."

As the counselor predicted, the incident caused an uproar. The guilty were given failing grades for the assignment. A few years later the counselor moved up the district ladder. The teacher was passed over several times for a permanent job.

Pilate, too, had a choice to make: stand up for what he knew was right, or cave in to a crowd who wanted him to set a mean-spirited murderer free and condemn an innocent man to death.

"But I find no fault in him," Pilate told the crowd, pointing to the man he knew had done nothing wrong.

"If you let this man go, you are no friend of Caesar," they shouted back. And Pilate did want to stay on the emperor's good side. So the guilty went free and the innocent was crucified.

Sometimes life just isn't fair. Even when we do the right thing. Justice is rarely served in this world. Someday, though, we'll all appear before the judgment seat of Christ to receive our due for the things we've done while on earth (2 Corinthians 5:10).

Only then will foul be foul and fair be fair.

When the unfairness of life threatens to overwhelm me, O Lord, give me the strength to keep doing what is right in Your sight. Amen.

MORE TEA: Read and meditate on John 18:28–40; 19:1–16.

Which Side of the Cross?

Whoever believes in the Son has eternal life, but whoever rejects the Son will not see life, for God's wrath remains on him. –John 3:36 NIV

HE WAS HANGING THERE, blood running from the gaping holes in his hands and feet, where huge iron nails held him to the wooden beam, when through the fog of pain he heard shouting. A mob followed a thin, blood-smeared man stumbling up the hill.

Another one. Wonder what He did. Blood oozed from deep gashes across the new man's back and poured down His face. The man on the cross opened his eyes wider. Wasn't this that prophet who rode into town on a donkey while the crowds cheered? Well, they were mocking Him now.

"You who are going to destroy the Temple and rebuild it in three days, save Yourself!"

"Come down from that cross, and then we'll believe You!"

Something clicked in his mind. *I remember. Miracles follow this man. What's His name? Ah, yes, Jesus—one who saves.*

The man on the cross on the other side of Jesus joined in the crowd's tirade.

"Aren't You the Christ?" he sneered. "Then save Yourself and us!"

He turned his head to the sneering thief.

"Don't you fear God?" he gasped. "We're getting what we deserve. But this man has done nothing wrong."

His eyes rested on the man on the middle cross. "Jesus, remember me when You come into Your kingdom."

Jesus turned his head and gazed at him, love shining through the pain in His eyes.

"I tell you the truth," Jesus told him, "today you will be with Me in Paradise."

"Those two men who . . . died alongside Jesus are representative of all mankind," wrote Chuck Colson. "We either recognize our sinful selves, our sentence of death, and our deserving that sentence, which leads us to repent and believe—or we curse God and die."

Which side of the cross are you on?

Jesus, Savior, thank You for what You did on the cross. Amen.

MORE TEA: Read and meditate on Luke 23:39–43.

Jesus' Cross

Even in the darkest night,
When I just turn and toss,
When all seems hopeless, nothing's right,
I remember Jesus' cross.

That beam of lumber cut to size,
Too heavy to be borne
By One who stepped to Calvary's call
Beaten, mocked, and scorned.

In the shadow of that cross,
How can I complain?
I have not sweat great drops of blood,
I've not endured such pain.

I've had no nails pierce tender flesh,
And no one's spit on me.
No soldier's opened up my back,
Nor stabbed my side with glee.

No jeering crowd shouts, "Crucify!"
Such loneliness I can't feel.
Yet love for me was the reason why
He bled, and I was healed.

The Time in the Tomb

Stop judging by the way things look. —John 7:24 ERV

JESUS WAS DEAD. What now?

They'd believed He was the Messiah, the Promised One, the Son of God. Divine. He'd healed the sick, raised the dead, cast out evil spirits, fed crowds of thousands with a few loaves of bread and a couple of fish, walked on water, calmed storms. He was their friend, their teacher, their master, their Lord.

How could this have happened? More important, how could He have let this happen? His enemies had had the last word. So everyone thought. Now what would happen to them?

I think about that day between Jesus' death and His resurrection.

His body lay in a cold, dark, dank tomb, buried in haste by a rich disciple who also happened to be a member of the very council that condemned Him to death. His disciples were locked away in an upper room, cowering in fear, wondering if they'd be next. Best stay hidden.

His enemies visited the Roman governor and asked him to post a guard at the tomb, "lest His disciples come by night and steal Him away, and say to the people, 'He has risen from the dead.' So the last deception will be worse than the first."

Yes, the time in the tomb was bleak. The disciples' dreams of a Messianic kingdom were gone, bled out by the nails that pierced His hands and feet. The last shred of hope pierced by the spear that plunged into His side as He hung on the cross.

But all was not as it seemed. It never is, is it?

We cannot see what God has in mind. We can only trust that He's got this, and He knows what He's doing. That eventually His plan and purpose will be fulfilled. We just have to wait it out.

Wait and pray. Wait and hope. Wait and fluctuate between fear and faith. Between despair and hope.

And waiting is the hardest part. It tests our faith, runs roughshod over what hope we're left clinging to. It stirs up doubt. Does God really care about little me? Is He ever going to make something good happen?

But it's in the cold, dark, dank tomb that our faith, through trial and testing, strengthens and grows. It doesn't grow in the good times, when euphoria and adrenaline feed our emotions.

Faith isn't about emotions, is it?

Faith isn't about what we think, is it?

Faith, to paraphrase a favorite quote, is like driving at night in the fog (or heavy rain). You can only see as far as your headlights' beam, but you can make the whole trip that way.

My friend and sister-in-Christ Laverne has lain in a coma since a speeding car hit her and sent her careening headfirst onto the pavement over Labor Day weekend, 2017. For more than a year friends prayed faithfully for a miracle.

I prayed. But, like the disciples, I doubted. There were seven months of nothing. Her time—and our time—in the tomb.

But just before Easter 2018 a thought came, unbidden: "Wouldn't Easter be the perfect time for God to bring this precious lady of faith out of her tomb?" I pushed it aside. After all, look at the facts. Even the doctors said there was no hope. And even if her body survived, her mind wouldn't.

Then I got a message from her husband: "Today Laverne was alert, with one eye open, squeezing my hand. Actually moved her hand sideways. When I got there, the nurse that shifts her position said Laverne was actually helping her move. (Never happened before.) Small miracles, slow but adding up. Thanks for continued prayers."

Shame on me. I'm too much like Thomas. I want to see before I believe. But I have to believe before I can truly see.

Are you in a tomb?

Have faith. Cling to that last thread of hope. Sunday's coming. New life will explode out of that tomb.

Lord, I believe. Help my unbelief. Amen.

MORE TEA: Read and meditate on Matthew 27:57–66.

Silent Saturday

Weeping may endure for a night, but joy cometh in the morning. –
Psalm 30:5 KJV

AS A CHILD I faithfully attended Holy Thursday and Good Friday services. One of the things I remember about this time right before Easter is that no music was played in church. The organ was silent, as were the bells and other instruments. Songs were sung *a cappella*.

This period of silence impressed upon me the solemnness of the time when God's Son was betrayed, condemned, crucified, and buried, paying the price for the sins of all mankind from the dawn of creation to the end of time.

I knew, of course, what would follow—Easter! The day Jesus burst out of that Mid-Eastern tomb in all His glory—alive forever! The return of music! The return of hope and joy.

Little, if anything, is said in the Gospels about Silent Saturday. For the Jews of that time, it was the Sabbath, a day of rest, a day no work was to be done.

We read nothing of what Jesus' followers did that day.

We can only imagine what they felt: grief, hopelessness, despair, terror. If the Jewish authorities could do this to Jesus, who performed all those miracles and claimed to be God's Son, what would they do to His disciples? So they hid, their dreams for the Kingdom and their places in it shattered, their future uncertain. The plan, they thought, went horribly, horribly wrong.

Or did it?

They had no idea that actually everything was going wonderfully, impossibly, exactly according to plan—God's plan. They didn't know they were not in the hiding place but in the waiting room between deep despair and unbridled joy. Between apparent defeat and glorious triumph. Between terror and a holy boldness that would set the world on fire and launch the Jesus Movement.

But, oh! That first Easter morning—who could even begin to describe the wonder they experienced at the empty tomb, the joy at seeing Jesus alive? It was exceedingly, abundantly, above all they could have imagined.

But they didn't know all that on Silent Saturday.

What about you?

Are you in a Silent Saturday time of your life? Are you dealing with grief, loss, bitter disappointment, discouragement, night-long weeping? Are you scraping at the bottom of the empty barrel of hope? Fighting despair and feel like you're losing the battle? Thinking that your dreams, your future, are sealed up in a tomb of decay?

Hang on, dear one loved by God. Saturday will pass. The night of weeping will end. The Son will burst over the horizon,

His rays chasing away despair and flooding your soul with hope and joy.

It's Silent Saturday, but get ready, Pilgrim. Sunday's coming.

Thank You, God, for Easter, when hope springs eternal. Amen.

MORE TEA: Read and meditate on John 16:16–33.

Easter

See! The winter is past;
the rains are over and gone.
Flowers appear on the earth;
the season of singing has come.

–Song of Songs 2:11–12 NIV

The Easter It Snowed

*But these are written that you may believe that Jesus is the Christ,
the Son of God, and that by believing, you may have life in his name. –
John 20:31 NIV*

EASTER FOR ME AS a child meant a new outfit, which included
a spring-like dress, shiny new shoes, and, although I've come to
abhor hats, a frilly Easter bonnet that would give the prettiest
girl in our class a run for her money. Easter was time to put
away the heavy, dark winter coat and bring out the lightweight,
pastel-colored one. It also meant brightly dyed eggs, jelly beans,
chocolate, and homemade bread and Easter cheese, which we
called *cirak*.

One year we spent Easter weekend at our cabin in the mountains near Cook Forest. Easter was early that year—the last
weekend in March, if I recall correctly. We'd found a small
country church a few miles away, so Mom packed our Easter
clothes. I grew up in southwestern Pennsylvania, where the
weather is much more spring-like even in late March than in
the mountains. We awoke that Sunday morning to blowing
snow and frigid temperatures. I shivered all through the church

service in my fancy dress, white anklets, patent leather shoes, and short jacket. I never forgot the Easter it snowed.

Now that I live in the western Pennsylvania mountains, I know not to put away the winter wardrobe too soon. The daffodils will bow under the snow, and tree leaves won't appear until mid-May. It doesn't matter whether Easter comes at the end of March or the end of April—we still can get snow.

I grew up associating Easter with spring and with blooming flowers and greening trees. Now I know a different truth: sometimes winter doesn't want to let go.

Focusing on a new Easter outfit or the long-anticipated arrival of spring, however, is focusing on the wrong thing. It's easy to forget what Easter is really all about, which is the celebration of Jesus' resurrection.

Because He conquered death, we, too, can conquer death. "I am the resurrection and the life," He told Martha before bringing her dead brother Lazarus back to life. "He who believes in Me, though he may die, shall live. And whoever lives and believes in Me shall never die. Do you believe this?" (John 11:25 NIV).

Easter means much more than a goodie basket and competing with the prettiest girl in class for the frilliest dress. Easter means much more than warm weather, flowers, and green grass.

It means the winter of the soul has lost its grip.

Because Jesus conquered death, I can experience an internal, eternal spring: "Now we look inside, and what we see is that anyone united with the Messiah gets a fresh start, is created new. The old life is gone; a new life burgeons! Look at it!" (2 Corinthians 5:17, The Message).

Snow on Easter? So what? It's always spring inside my heart.

Lord, let me see the flowers beneath the snow. Amen.

MORE TEA: Read and meditate on John 20.

Mother's Day

Charm is deceptive, and beauty is fleeting,
but a woman who fears the LORD is to be praised.

–Proverbs 31:30 NIV

Mama's Hankie

I wasn't always tattered;
I wasn't always torn.
I didn't always look so limp,
So tired and forlorn.
Once my threads were crisper,
My colors seemed to glow;
But I was harsh against a face
When tears would start to flow.

So I traded in my beauty
For softer threads of years,
So I could fit into your hand
And gather all your tears.
So treasure all my careworn threads—
In time they'll fall apart;
And take with you the tenderness
And love that's in my heart.

Remembering Mom

Her children rise up and call her blessed. –Proverbs 31:28 ESV

MY MOTHER WASN'T THE cuddly, "warm fuzzy" type. She was a strict disciplinarian who found joy in family, faith, hard work, and music.

She didn't need an alarm clock to awaken her at five a.m. Her biological clock did it for her. She woke up wound up, kept wound up with pots of coffee, and finally wound down after the dinner dishes were done.

Back then, there were no dishwashers, automatic washers, and clothes dryers. Dishes, pots, and pans were washed and dried by hand, then put away as soon as the meal was done. Clothes were washed in a wringer washer and hung on a line to dry. When the weather was cooperative, they sashayed in the outside breeze (after a finger-wagging to heaven from my mom—"Now don't You let it rain!"). When it wasn't clothes-drying weather, they hung from wire lines strung through the basement.

Mom never left a job for the next day, unless it was a major project, such as knocking old plaster off a wall with a crowbar to prepare it for new plaster. She could snore away on the sofa in peace every evening because her work for the day was done.

Paydays meant trips to the bank, the grocery store, the utility company, and wherever else money was owed or something needed—and she walked because she didn't drive. Dad tried to teach her, but she ran the car into a telephone pole and refused to get behind the wheel again. We used no credit cards. If the store extended credit, the bill was paid in full on payday.

She did not have a job outside the home. Her house and family were her job. She was the family accountant and, because of her childhood poverty, knew how to stretch a dollar. So when Dad was laid off, she knew how to tighten our belts, using toilet paper for facial tissues and serving meatless meals, such as bowties and cottage cheese or tomato soup and grilled cheese sandwiches—still two of my favorite meals today.

Technology was on the distant horizon. No one was tethered to an electronic device 24/7, so I had time to learn to play the piano, visit with Baba (my grandmother) across the street, go to the library, and read to my heart's content.

Life was simpler. We were taught to obey and respect our parents and teachers. The leather strap lying in a kitchen drawer was to be avoided at all costs.

"A good name is more desirable than great riches; to be esteemed better than silver or gold" (Proverbs 22:1) was one of the Maddock family mottos, as well as "Honor your father and your mother" (Exodus 20:12).

I never realized how much my mother modeled the Proverbs 31 woman until I wrote this.

I only wish Mom were alive today so I could tell her, "Many women do noble things, Mom, but you surpassed them all. I love you. Thank you for teaching me, by example, how to be a wife, a mother, and a woman of character."

Help me, Lord, to be a Proverbs 31 woman. Amen.

MORE TEA: Read and meditate on Proverbs 31:1–31.

Letter to My Daughter

Direct your children onto the right path, and when they are older, they will not leave it. —Proverbs 22:6 NLT

Dearest Jaime,

It's been only thirty minutes since you left, but I missed you before you even pulled away from the house. . . .

I wrote that first sentence three hours ago. I thought I'd get my column in early, but I couldn't sit still. Couldn't focus. Couldn't think of anything but saying goodbye to you and the boys after your two-week visit home. So I started cleaning the house.

I hate to sound cliché, but where did those two weeks go? It seems like only yesterday that Dad was working until ten p.m. every evening to get enough of the back deck done so we could enjoy it while you were here. Was it three weeks ago that I washed windows, laundered curtains, and gave the house a good cleaning? That we stocked the pantry and refrigerator with more groceries than we'd bought in a month (or more)?

Brought the bunk mattresses from the motorhome and set up the boys' bedroom in my study?

It's been thirteen years since you moved down south, but the goodbyes haven't gotten any easier. One time, when the boys were still small, I found a tiny white sock scrunched up, inside out, in the bathroom as I cleaned the house after you left. I still have it—tacked to the bulletin board in my study. One of the treasures of this mother's heart.

That's how I deal with the sick goodbye feeling after you leave—I get busy, body in motion, making noise in a suddenly too-quiet house, allowing my mind and heart time to transition to "back to normal."

Dad and I are proud of you—you've come through the rough teen and young adult years shining as gold. You've overcome obstacles life has thrown at you with grit and gumption, like when I took you as a toddler to the doctor for your shots and you hopped up on the exam table, thrust out your arm, and looked him fearlessly in the eye, as if to say, "Go ahead, give it your best shot."

I've never heard you whine or complain that life was unfair. And some of the things life has thrown at you *were* unfair. But you rose above them all and have done marvelously well—receiving the college's "Heart of Gold" award for your work with the support group for parents with kids who are autistic, graduating *cum laude* after seven years as part-time and full-time student while starting your family and dealing with a child who was eventually diagnosed as autistic. Yet today, there are few signs of autism. Because you fought for him.

I can still see you and Adam at the dining room table after putting the boys to bed, math and science textbooks scattered around you.

There's so much more I want to say, but I simply don't have the words to express the love that overflows from my heart to yours—and how blessed I am to have you for a daughter.

Love,
Mom

Thank You, Lord, for my precious daughter and her family. Thank you for Your hand on her life. Amen.

MORE TEA: Read and meditate on Deuteronomy 6:5–9.

First Corinthians 13 for Mothers

THOUGH I MAY SPEAK the jargon of professors, doctors, and ministers, if I can't speak so that my own children understand me, then all I do is make educated noise.

Even if I was known as a scholar or a person with mountain-moving faith, unless my children could truly say, "Mommy loves me!", then I am nothing.

And although I save Campbell's labels for missions, distribute food boxes to the needy, make a dish for a funeral dinner, give used clothing to the local homeless shelter; even though I carry a signed organ donor card, if I don't lovingly look to the needs of my own children, all other good works will profit me nothing.

I need to be patient with their immature thinking, stupid mistakes, and know-it-all attitudes; and show kindness in the face of whining, arguing, and pouting. I need to love them as they are, not as I expect them to be. I cannot envy the parent whose child is a better scholar, musician, or athlete than I perceive my child to be. Yet neither should I vaunt my own child's successes, for to do so would put the burden of proof on my child, who will strive to live up to my sometimes unrealistic expectations, and perhaps never feel good enough.

I should not be rude to my children, even in my own home, where I long to let my hair down, not snap at them when I'm feeling tired or pressured. I need to give them the same respect I give others and be considerate of their feelings, their privacy, their possessions, and even (shudder) their rooms!

I should not keep a tally of my children's wrongs, and then triumphantly flourish it at a time when it's convenient for me. To gently show them when and why they are wrong is more effective than harsh punishment that doesn't fit the crime and serves only to crush their spirits. Insisting my way is the only way will stiffen their resistance, but teaching them right from wrong by example and praying for discernment may someday lead to rejoicing when my children follow the truth.

With God's help I will never give up believing in them, knowing that He who created them has a wonderful plan for their lives and will complete what He started. Even when they respond to the pull of the world, I will rest on the promise that God's Word never returns void. They cannot stray so far that my love and prayers cannot follow.

Genuine love outlasts parental sermons that they quickly forget. Even if I was able to understand insurance policies and all the legalese in which they are written, what good would it do my children if I had no love for them?

I must remember that I, too, was once a child. What wisdom and knowledge I have now were acquired with painful experience.

I must remember that God alone knows their hearts. I see only the outward appearance and assume way too much. Someday God's plan for each of their lives will unfold like a beautiful flower, and I will understand the trials that seem so hard to get through now.

Faith, hope, and love are the foundation blocks upon which I build my relationship with my children. But the strongest, most enduring block of all is love.

MORE TEA: Read and meditate on 1 Corinthians 13.

A Mother's Prayer

And Jesus grew in wisdom and stature, and in favor with God and men. –Luke 2:52 NIV

MY CHILDREN ARE ALL grown, now, Lord. I don't hear their voices every day. I don't have to cook for them, pick up after them, or remind them to clean their rooms, take out the garbage, do their homework, or be home by curfew.

No more do I scrutinize report cards or attend teacher conferences, holiday programs, and piano and ballet recitals. No schedules deck my refrigerator.

I don't have to answer "why" questions or make sure I have the right change for lunch money or explain why I don't want another dog.

My day no longer centers around them. They are all on their own, except one, who, in college, is almost on his own. I sure hope I've done a good job.

But, Lord, my job is far from over. Now I get to parent from my knees. Now I get to practice heartfelt, persistent prayer.

I pray that they would be RICH—not in the worldly sense, but in the character traits that will bring them success and satisfaction as human beings:

R – RESPECT: That they would respect themselves, others, and You. That they would command the respect of others by their behavior and beliefs.

RESPONSIBLE: That they would fulfill their commitments and duties without whining or complaining. That they would be accountable for their own foul-ups and not look for excuses or try to place the blame on circumstances or others.

RESOURCEFUL: In this spendthrift, credit-laden society, that they would realize that it's okay to shop at Goodwill and it's not necessary to buy brand names. That they would use wisely the resources of time, talent, and treasure.

I – INTEGRITY: That they would be persons who keep their word and do the right thing, even if they must stand alone and go against the flow. That they would be fair and just.

INTELLIGENCE: That they would develop the brains You gave them and use good judgment.

INDUSTRY: That they would not be afraid of good, old-fashioned hard work, and not be ashamed to get their hands dirty doing it.

C – CHARACTER: That they would have high standards for their behavior and speech, and find the inner strength to do what is right through a personal relationship with You.

COMPASSION: That they would look out for the other guy, be their brothers' keepers, help the helpless, and fight for the underdog. That they would nurture an unselfish spirit. That they would know that kindness is not weakness, but strength.

CHEERFULNESS: That they would seek and find joy everywhere they go, and leave it behind them. That they would look on the bright side and make a smile part of their daily wardrobe. Give them a sense of humor, Lord, for that is one of the best shock absorbers of life.

H – HONESTY/HONOR: That they would always tell the truth and do what is right, and strive to be the person described in Psalm 1.

HUMILITY: That they would not think themselves better than anyone else and not treat others as their servants.

HUNGER: That they would hunger and thirst after You, and seek You with all of their hearts. That they would cultivate a personal relationship with You through Your Son, that they would grow in grace and knowledge of Jesus as Savior and Lord. That they would read and study Your Word. That they would know, love, and serve You with the talents You have blessed them with.

Guide them in the problems they face and in the decisions they make. Bless them and keep them, Lord, and make Your face shine upon them. Show them Your grace and favor and give them peace (Numbers 6:24–26).

MORE TEA: Read and meditate on Psalm 1.

Hippie Days Are Here—Again?

"I'M GOING TO BE a hippie for Halloween this year," my daughter, Jaime, announced when she was sixteen. "Do you have any old bell bottoms?"

I shook my head. What was this challenging teenager up to now?

"I think Dad used those for grease rags years ago," I said.

As she disappeared into the attic, I reflected on the outgoing little girl I once cuddled in my lap. In her place was this headstrong teenager who wanted privileges I wasn't ready to give.

Help me, Lord, I'd pray, *I don't know what to do with her.* I grounded her often, rarely believed anything she told me, and checked up on her everywhere she went. *Was I this difficult to raise?*

Jaime descended from the attic with a skirt I'd made for her when she was five and an Indian girl for Halloween.

"Don't you think it's too short?" I suggested. She grinned, green eyes twinkling.

"Well," I sighed, shaking my head in resignation, "wear your cheerleading tights underneath."

"What kind of shoes should I wear?" She was off and running now. For once I hadn't disapproved. I thought about the black suede platform shoes I'd bought when I was a slim, young thing. For a moment I almost regretted giving those impractical style statements to Goodwill.

"What about boots?" she asked, taking off through the house in search of footwear. She returned with a pair of black, combat-style hunting boots.

"Would these work?" she asked, pulling one on. Her older brother Todd sneered.

"Hippies burned those things," he informed her, his voice dripping with sarcastic authority. "They *protested* war, remember?"

"Oh," she said, ignoring his aren't-you-the-idiot tone and dropping the boot on the floor.

While Jaime dug into a pile of shoes, Todd opened the coat closet and pulled out a worn brown suede jacket with fringe.

"Here!" he said, thrusting it at her. "If you really want to look like a hippie, wear this!"

She slipped it over her black, form-fitting jersey.

"That's the perfect finishing touch!" I exclaimed, scrutinizing her brown leather sandals, Indian-style miniskirt, and matching headband. She grinned and held up both hands in a peace sign. Silky chestnut hair fell to her shoulders and framed her dimpled cheeks.

Did I look like that? I wondered. *Everyone says she looks just like me when I was her age.*

"Do you remember where I got that jacket?" my husband said.

"Tijuana, Mexico, when you were in the service," I answered, remembering a frosty, moonlit hayride and the smell of new leather and old hay mixed.

I'd met him a couple of months after his discharge. By then he'd grown a beard and sported wavy, shoulder-length hair. I fell in love with him when he smiled and his blue eyes twinkled. But my mother doubted this tall, shaggy man who took me for rides on his Harley was the man for me—until she saw the twinkle in his eyes when she confessed looking for needle marks on his arm.

"I need some hippie jewelry," Jaime said. "Do you have any beads? What kind of earrings did they wear? She spun around and scooted upstairs, returning with one gold earring dangling from one ear and a big, gold hoop in the other.

"Which ones?" she asked.

"The dangly ones," I said.

"The hoops," said her father. "I think I have a peace sign necklace around here someplace that you can wear."

I rolled my eyes. Now *he* was getting into the act! But then, wasn't it fun? For once mother and daughter weren't locking horns. Caught up in the excitement of dressing her up, I remembered what it was like to be young and struggling to find my own identity. The years melted away, and it was I who stood before scrutinizing parents.

"Please, give me the freedom to make my own mistakes!" My own words echoed in my daughter's eyes. Now I was the one holding on too tightly. *Just love her,* I sensed God telling me. *Rejoice in the person she is becoming.*

"Yes," I smiled at my hippie-wanna-be. "A peace sign would be just perfect."

Lessons from Mom

Mary quietly treasured these things in her heart and often thought about them. –Luke 2:19 TLB

ONE SUMMER DAY WHEN I was quite young, my mother was hosing off the sidewalk beside the house and accidentally sprayed a bird. Now, birds are a dime a dozen, right? What's one less bird in the scheme of things? But she was so distraught, she cradled the little thing in her cupped hands, praying it would survive. I don't remember whether or not it did, but I do remember her distress. Her compassion that day taught me that *all creatures matter.*

Then there was the time she caught me behind the sofa pretending to smoke one of her cigarettes.

"If I catch you again," she warned, "I'm going to light it."

"You go right ahead," I said.

When I finally caught my breath after gagging over the kitchen sink for an eternity, I determined I would never smoke. And I never have. But what would have been the outcome if she hadn't made good on her warning? She taught me *to follow through,* to do what you say you're going to do, even when it's difficult.

Then there was the time I invited my entire class to my house one Saturday for my birthday party and didn't tell her. I knew she'd say no, and I really, really, really wanted a party like all the other kids had.

I bowled on Saturday mornings, and that day I plodded home, worried that I'd become the laughingstock of the class when they showed up to my nonparty. But the house was decorated and a large cake adorned the table. Mom had discovered my chicanery—and I didn't get grounded for life, either. That day I learned *what mercy was.*

Fast forward about a dozen years. Mom and I were flying to Alabama to spend Christmas with my brother. For the trip I dressed in a red velour miniskirt and matching short-waist top, stockings, and dress shoes. Since my brother was deprived of the Slovak dishes he grew up on, Mom took a casserole full of frozen homemade pierogies. Somehow I became the guardian of the goodies. Perhaps the image of my bird-like, aging mother lugging a lump of frost from Pittsburgh to Montgomery overcame my need to appear chic.

In Atlanta we had to rush to get to the next gate in time. Somewhere between Eastern and Delta I realized my carefully donned image was gone with the wind. I learned more than one lesson that day: to dress for the occasion, wear comfortable clothes when traveling, and that *a mother's love transcends everything,* even practicality.

More images flood my mind: Mom, dish towel thrown over her shoulder, singing next to the piano, her foot tapping the hardwood floor while my sister played a tune she loved. She taught me *music is a balm to the soul,* a buffer in the storms of life.

I remember her lighting a vigil light daily and praying after she'd hung the laundry on the outside line, "God, don't You let it rain." She taught me that *faith makes a difference* even in the little, day-to-day things.

Ah . . . all things she taught me by just being herself. How blessed I am!

Thank You, God, for my mother and the lessons she taught me, even if she did embarrass me at times. Amen.

MORE TEA: Read and meditate on Deuteronomy 6:6–7.

My Cookbook Treasures

But Mary kept all these things, and pondered them in her heart. –
Luke 2:19 NKJV

MY SISTER GAVE ME my first cookbook in 1972. I'd just graduated from college, landed my first real job, and set up housekeeping in my very own apartment—much to my mother's disappointment. Mom wanted me to find a job back home and live with her. My father had died less than a year earlier.

"You won't have to cook, clean, or do laundry," she said. "Think of the money you'd save on rent."

I wasn't even tempted. We were too much alike: independent, I'll-do-it-myself, stay-out-of-my-way-while-I'm-doing-this kind of women. When I was growing up, all I was allowed to do in her kitchen was make tea and popcorn, and, once in a great while, macaroni and cheese.

So, you see, I didn't really know how to cook. Hence the cookbook was a perfect graduation gift.

The first time I used it was when I wanted to make hot dogs for supper. Was I supposed to boil them or fry them? Or both?

So I pulled out my new (and only) cookbook and looked up "hot dogs." I found a dozen ways to cook hot dogs, none of which seemed right. But I was too proud to call home, so I chose the simplest recipe: I boiled them for five to eight minutes, wrapped them in slices of cheese and bread, then broiled them. It still wasn't what I remembered Mom doing, but it was edible.

Betty Crocker and I had only just begun. My next feat was spaghetti sauce, which I had simmering on the old gas range when this really neat guy I'd just met came to my apartment for the first time. I offered him some spaghetti, cautioning him, "This is the first time I've ever made it."

"I was in the service," he said. "I can eat anything."

He's been eating "anything" for forty-five years now.

Over time Betty Crocker taught me how to make pie crust, potato salad, biscuits, pancakes, cookies, chicken, lasagna, egg salad, and tuna salad, just to name a few dishes.

More than four decades of use have taken their toll on my cookbook. A giant rubber band holds it together, and keeps its red hardback covers in place and all the stuff stuffed between its pages. The masking tape, now yellowed and dried out, stopped doing the job long ago.

Stuffed between its grease-splattered, stained pages are recipes from other sources—most of which I've never used and probably will never use. But I keep just in case.

And, curiously, cards, notes, and mementoes of my life. Why on earth I saved these in my cookbook, I have no idea. But there they are—a VBS certificate of recognition between the pancakes and waffles pages; handmade Christmas and Easter cards and decorations, a birthday card to my husband from our youngest, signed "I love you, DaDDy" in his childhood scrawl, a homemade Christmas card from this same son, who, for some reason, signed it with his first and last name; Mother's Days cards, Father's Day cards, Valentine's Day cards, a postcard sent from our oldest when he went to a summer camp, assuring us in faded red pencil that he took his medicine and that he was in better shape than we thought—and that the cooking was bad, but he had two helpings. Another letter from summer camp, this one from our daughter, who told us her dance classes were hard but fun, the showers cold, she loved us "a bunch," and we could get her address from the "pamflitt."

Another card from our oldest, again at summer camp, telling us that "I like it up here. I got sick on the frist day." Also stuffed in the cookbook are directions on how to take care of our grandson when we babysat and a handmade book of "Mother's Day Promises," one promise per page: "I will always do the trim mowing, the dishes, clean my room, make breakfast on Sundays, and walk the baby." Only two were marked as done.

Another note from camp from the oldest: "I miss you. Show Dad my tree cabin. P.S. Teel Daivid I love him. P.P.S. Teel Jaime I love her." An In Memoriam card from my brother-in-law's funeral. A Christmas card from my mother—I think it was the last card she signed and sent before Alzheimer's got the best of her.

Occasionally when I'm leafing through the cookbook—I have a shelf of them now, but this is the only one that I save stuff in—I'll come across one of these treasures. I'll smile as I read the words, running my finger across them lightly, then hold it close to my heart, holding back the tears that fill my eyes.

These days, I'm a lot like my cookbook—falling apart on the outside, but on the inside, stuffed with more love and joy than my heart can hold.

Dear God, thank You for my family—they are the key ingredients in the recipe for a life of love. Amen.

MORE TEA: Read and meditate on Proverbs 31:10–31.

My Many Mothers

They can train the younger women. —Titus 2:4 NIV

ON MOTHER'S DAY WE honor those women who carried us in their bodies, gave birth to us in pain, hauled us around on their hips, kissed our boo-boos, cheered for us when we were losing, stood up to the bullies, welcomed our friends (even the ones they knew were dirty rats), protected us when we thought we didn't need protection, disciplined us when we defied them, sought us when we strayed, released us when we were ready, prayed for us constantly, and loved us unflinchingly even when we were mean, rotten, nasty, and cruel.

They glimpsed in us what we couldn't recognize and nurtured the kernel of talent no one else saw. Our dreams became their dreams, and, come hell or high water, they would see to it that we had every opportunity to make them come true. When we fell, they picked us up, dusted us off, and sent us on our way again. Sometimes we thought they were being mean and unreasonable, but when we became parents ourselves, we began to understand.

I have spiritual mothers, too—those older, more experienced women who nurture me on my faith journey. Who, by their example, teach me what it means to be a Christian woman.

Mary took me under her wing when I was but a babe in Christ. Her invitation to a Christian Women's Club luncheon led to Bible studies, service, and Christian friendships I treasure to this day, forty years later.

Joan (pronounced "Jo-Ann") opened her home—a hive of activity with five daughters—for a Bible study, where I found room to grow. Her words, "I learned to hold the panic in," were my stay when my husband carried in our five-year-old son wrapped in a sheet, blood streaming from his head. That day I learned not only to hold the panic in, but also that cuts to the scalp bleed profusely because of all the hair follicles.

Caroline's love of life poured from her generous, servant heart. "If the Lord came today," she said once, giggling, "I'd tell him I can't go. I've got too much to do!"

Louise's unquenchable zest for life, unflinching faith, and passion for God fueled a life of tireless service. Just remembering her constant smile and hearty laughter blesses me and encourages me to keep on keeping on.

And, finally, Dorothy. A woman whose love for God, life of prayer, undaunted faith, and kind heart drew me to her like a parched traveler to a fresh mountain stream. When she was diagnosed with advanced cancer, I despaired until she said: "Don't give up on me!" What faith!

To paraphrase John Donne, "No woman is an island." Our lives are an ongoing stream in the course of time, one life touching another, touching another, touching another, on and on, until time is no more.

Whose life has touched yours? Whose life is yours touching?

Thank You, Lord, for the women whose lives have blessed mine. May I, in turn, touch others' lives for You. Amen.

MORE TEA: Read and meditate on Titus 2:1, 3–5.

Memorial Day

Greater love has no one than this,
than to lay down one's life for his friends.

–John 15:13 NKJV

Never the Same

Greater love has no one than this, that he lay down his life for his friends. –John 15:13 NIV

MY FATHER WAS WOUNDED on the pitiful island of Attu in World War II. Shrapnel embedded in his spine left him paralyzed, recuperating in a VA hospital for a year. He was never the same.

The spinal injuries he suffered defending a little spit of volcanic rock hanging on the tail end of the Aleutian Islands off the coast of Alaska left him with recurrent back pain for the rest of his life. When the first symptoms of stomach cancer appeared thirty years later, he thought it was his troublesome back. By the time the cancer was discovered, it was too late. He died a month after surgery.

My mother was never the same. I was never the same.

War does that. It changes lives, steals dreams, shatters hopes. But the men and women who returned from World War II were stalwart characters. They got on with life, building families and communities. They were the first in line at the polls on election day, first in line at a Red Cross blood drive. They understood duty, loyalty, courage. They didn't preach it, they lived it. Their priorities were—in order—God, family, country.

Dad refused to talk about the war. So when I discovered his Bronze Star hidden in a dresser drawer, I was surprised. I didn't think Attu was significant enough to warrant a medal for bravery. One World War II writer described it as "the lonesomest spot this side of hell."

But, unknown to the American public, for fifteen months—from early June 1942 to the mid-August 1943—US forces fought off a Japanese invasion in what one writer described as "arduous operations hampered by shortages afloat, ashore, and in the air . . . not to mention the almost insuperable obstacles of weather and terrain." When it was all over, American casualties added up to 3,829 (25 percent of the invading force—second only in proportion to Iwo Jima): 549 dead, 1,148 injured, 1,200 with injuries from the severe cold, 614 with disease, and 318 to miscellaneous causes. The Japanese lost 2,351 men; only 28 were taken prisoner.[*]

Attu didn't get much press. It was only as I looked up information for this column that I discovered the real significance of this historic battle.

We still were reeling from Pearl Harbor, as the Aleutian Island invasion took place a mere six months later. Perhaps it was to protect the public, to prevent a panic, that news about the battle raging in the Bering Sea was blacked out. How many outside the military and the government knew at the time that the enemy was that close? Our military was tied up in Europe and the South Pacific. Little Attu paled in comparison.

Yet history would have been different had we lost Attu and the rest of the Aleutian Islands.

Never once in all his pain did my father ever complain or protest war. He knew the price that must be paid for freedom. Whether in Vietnam, Bosnia, or the Middle East, liberty's price is the blood of our sons and daughters—no less than what God paid for our freedom from sin and its consequences.

Our eternal history would have been different had the battle for our souls not been waged and won two thousand years ago on a godforsaken spit of land called Calvary. But this war, unlike human wars, changes lives for the better, restores dreams, and renews hope. Once we decide whose side we're on, we are never the same.

For God so loved the world that He gave His only Son, so that everyone who believes in Him will not perish but have eternal life (John 3:16 NLT). Thank you, thank you, thank you, God! Amen.

*Source:
http://www.hlswilliwaw.com/aleutians/Aleutians/html/aleutians-wwii.htm

Daddy and the Poppies

Greater love has no one than this, that he lay down his life for his friends. –John 15:13 NIV

ONE OF THE EARLIEST memories I have is of my father "buying" me a poppy from a man in a military uniform outside our church on a Sunday morning. As I grew older, I came to understand when Dad put money in the can, he was donating to a local veterans' organization.

A World War II veteran of the US Army, my father didn't talk about his service. How I wish I would have asked more questions! But I was young with my own life ahead of me, and had little, if any, interest in something that didn't directly affect me.

Now I regret that selfish attitude. At sixty-seven, I realize my roots are as important as my wings. I have plenty of questions now. Where was he stationed? What was his Army job? I know he'd attained the rank of sergeant but little else. I may never know this side of eternity. My parents, and that generation of relatives who could have given me answers, are all gone now.

I wrote to the Veteran's Administration for my dad's service records, but unfortunately a fire destroyed them. I researched "Attu" online and learned that, had the Japanese won that historic battle on the westernmost Aleutian island, we may well have fought World War II on continental American soil. I sent for the DVD of the PBS documentary *Red, White, Black, and Blue*, "a wrenching look at a forgotten battle."

But I'd rather have the story from my father's point of view. It would mean so much more to me.

So every year, in memory of my father, I get a poppy and entwine it on my purse. If I have a grandchild with me, I get one for them, too.

"My daddy—your great-grandfather—always got me a poppy," I say. "Do you know where the idea for poppies came from?"

Then I tell them about the poem written by Lt. Col. John McCrae in 1915, during World War I: "In Flanders Fields the poppies blow / Between the crosses row on row."

I tell them about Moina Michael, who, in response to McCrae's poem, went out and bought a bouquet of poppies and distributed them, asking that they be worn in tribute to the fallen. Donations were given to servicemen in need.

If I still have their attention—and I make sure I do—I recite the verse she penned: "We cherish, too, the poppy red / That grows on fields where valor led; / It seems to signal to the skies / That blood of heroes never dies, / But lends a luster to the red / Of the flower that blooms above the dead / In Flanders Field."

"And today," I say, concluding the brief history lesson, "red poppies are made by disabled veterans in hospitals, with the donations going to support a variety of veterans' organizations."

And then I give them a poppy.

Let not loyalty and faithfulness forsake you; bind them about your neck, write them on the tablet of your heart. –Proverbs 3:3 RSV

Father, let the poppy also remind us of the sacrifice Your Son made for our eternal freedom. Amen.

MORE TEA: Read and meditate on Proverbs 3:3.

Don't Forget to Remember

"In the future when your descendants ask their fathers, 'What do these stones, mean?' tell them . . ." – *Joshua 4:21–22 NIV*

WITH THREE GRANDCHILDREN ON different ball teams (one of them is an umpire), hubby and I are at the Punxsutawney Little League Fields just about every evening. After the sixth game in four days, I told Dean we should park our camper at the ball field.

The Punxsutawney Little League complex is almost a second home to us, as we spent many a summer afternoon and evening there when our youngest played baseball. Five well-maintained and lighted ball fields for Minor League, Little League, Senior Little League, what we call the "Teener League" (VFW), and girls' softball, are located beside Mahoning Creek.

Each ball field is named for someone local. Some honor those who have devoted much of their time to maintain and improve the fields and the league. Two fields are named as memorials.

The Little League field is called the Billy Titus Memorial Field, named after a Punxsutawney Little Leaguer who was killed in a farming accident.

The VFW League field, the Rich Kuntz Memorial Field, is named for SP4 Richard Lorraine Kuntz, who was killed in action in Vietnam on February 5, 1968, six weeks before his twenty-first birthday.

My grandson once asked me, "Who was Rich Kuntz? Why is the field named after him?" Since I've spent half a lifetime at the fields and know the stories behind the names, I was able to tell him. But it got me wondering: how many people drive right by those signs or even say the name of the ball field and don't realize the significance?

Memorials are built and named so we won't forget, so those who come after will learn of the sacrifice of the Vietnam soldier, the love a Little Leaguer who never got to play Senior League had for the game.

This weekend we observe Memorial Day, a day set aside to honor and remember our military men and women who gave their lives in service to our country.

Some died in action, some went missing in action and never were found, some died a slow death after they came home and tried to resume a normal life. Some are still alive, but they will never be the same.

Sadly, these holidays that are set aside to remember and honor those who have stepped to the plate for our country are too often perceived as simply a day off work, to relax, catch up on things, feast and frolic.

While there's nothing wrong with any of those activities, let us not forget to remember why we observe Memorial Day.

On the way to the ball field, there's a grassy field beside the road that's covered with US flags. Each time I passed it this week, more flags waved in the breeze. Yesterday, I slowed down to read the sign. Passersby are invited to place a free flag there in honor of a veteran.

I didn't have time to stop then, but the next day I made a special trip to that field and placed flags in honor of my loved ones who have served.

What about you? What are you doing to remember this Memorial Day?

Thank you, Lord, for those who gave themselves to serve, protect, and defend our country. Let us never forget the sacrifices they made. Amen.

MORE TEA: Read and meditate on Joshua 4.

Father's Day

He will take great delight in you,
he will quiet you with his love,
he will rejoice over you with singing.

–Zephaniah 3:17 NIV

Daddy's Girl

These commands I give you today are to be upon your hearts. Impress them on your children. Talk about them when you sit at home and when you walk along the road, when you lie down and when you get up. –Deuteronomy 6:7 NIV

I GREW UP IN Donora, then a steel mill town, one of many along the Monongahela River in the Mon Valley. Dad worked day shift at the mill, which was a fifteen-minute walk down the hill from our green wood-frame, two-story house on McCrea Avenue. When I heard the mill whistle signaling the end of his shift, I'd wait at the top of the path for him. To this day, I don't know whether I was more eager to see my father or discover what treat he had for me in his lunch bucket.

The youngest of three, I was "Daddy's girl." He was the one who named me. Mom wanted "Teresa," but Dad insisted, "Her name is Michele." No place was safer than his lap, nothing better than horseback rides on his strong back at bedtime. Although Dad was small in stature, he was a giant in my eyes. His off hours were spent in his carpentry shop, a more fun place for me than Mom's kitchen. While Dad crafted cabinets, I'd loop a clothesline rope around one end of a sawhorse, swing my leg over the back, and ride the trails of my imagination. My continuous questions never seemed to bother him. He answered every one patiently and in a way I could understand.

It was Dad who bought me my first tricycle. It was Dad who introduced me to archery and chuckled when he came home from work to discover one of my stray arrows had found its mark in one of his shop windows.

It was Dad who went looking for me one summer night when I was fifteen and didn't come home on time after an evening with friends at a church bazaar. Back then we didn't have cell phones, and I hadn't even given it a thought to let my parents know I was walking my best friend, who lived across town, home.

It was Dad, a year later, who taught me to drive. I can still hear his voice cautioning me to "watch out for the other guy." And when I'd climb the stairs at bedtime, I often found him sitting on the side of his bed, head bowed, hands folded in prayer.

It was Dad who saw to it that I'd never have to repay college loans. He'd paved the way for me to get funding through the state Bureau of Vocational Rehabilitation because of my hearing loss. I resented it at first—I didn't want to be "different"—but through the years I've come to appreciate it.

Although Dad didn't live to see my children (he died when I was a senior in college), the lessons he taught me by his example—lessons of patience, steadfast love, and the importance of family—will remain with me as long as I live.

Thank you, Lord, for a father who loved me the way I was and helped me, through his example, to become the person I am today. Amen.

MORE TEA: Read and meditate on Psalm 1.

Someday You'll Understand

Honor your father and your mother. –Exodus 20:12 NIV

I CAME ACROSS DAD'S letter while rummaging through the bookcase for some now-forgotten item. The slightly yellowed envelope bore a State College postmark. I smiled. I didn't even know I'd saved it.

Settling on the game room carpet as snowflakes whirled in the winter wind outside, I reverently unfolded the letter, typewritten on motel stationery.

"My dear Michele," it began. "Perhaps by now you are over the mad spell at me for scolding you the other night . . ."

My mind drifted back to a mid-summer night when I was fifteen. The warm summer sky sparkled with a thousand pinlights as my friends and I walked through town. It was just the kind of night that holds magic for a teenage girl on the brink of growing up. Heady with all the freedom and fun, I'd neglected to call my parents to tell them I'd be late. By the time I climbed the front porch steps, it was past midnight. Dad waited at the door.

"This is the first time you ever stayed out late without calling and letting me know your whereabouts," the letter continued. "I was actually sick with worry after walking up to the bazaar and not finding you there. By that time I was imagining everything."

I couldn't remember Dad ever being so angry with me before. After an angry scene, I stormed up to my bedroom, grounded for two weeks. The next day Dad seemed to have gotten over his anger, but I treated him with icy silence. By the time he left for work Monday morning, I still hadn't spoken to him. Since Dad worked out of town through the week, I knew I wouldn't see him until Friday. The letter came Wednesday.

As I read Dad's words that long-ago day, my stubborn resistance melted away as a father's love triumphed over teenage pride. One moment of panic, I realized, doesn't cancel out years of steadfast love. Four years later Dad died.

"It is so hard for a parent to be cross with a child, but sometimes it is necessary for your own good," he wrote. "Perhaps when you have children of your own, you will understand how we feel."

I thought of my own three children. They'd all had me frantic with worry and fear at times as I imagined the worst.

"Yes, Dad," I whispered softly, holding his letter close to my heart. "I understand."

Thank You, Father, for parents who loved me enough to discipline me when I needed it. Help me to be a parent worthy of being respected, valued, and honored. Amen.

MORE TEA: Read and meditate on Hebrews 12:5–11.

Setting the Bar

"Abba, Father, all things are possible for you." –Jesus, as quoted in Mark 14:36 ESV

For you did not receive the spirit of slavery to fall back into fear, but you received the Spirit of adoption as sons, by whom we cry, "Abba! Father!" –Romans 8:15 ESV

WHEN MY BROTHER PETE was in high school, he was returning home after a date when he ran into a stone wall. Now, it wasn't a tall, stone-and-mortar wall, but a short wall built with stones laid one on top of the other. The car didn't have much damage to it. After all, it was a 1957 Oldsmobile made of steel. In other words, it was a tank.

My brother woke my father up with the words, "Dad, I need you."

Why I remember this incident after more than fifty-four years, I have no idea. But the words "Dad, I need you" were imprinted indelibly on my mind.

I've been thinking about fathers and the roles they play in our lives. And about God as our heavenly Father.

Your perception of God as your Father is influenced by your own relationship with your earthly father. That's why people who experienced abusive fathers or have had a bad relationship with their earthly fathers have a difficult time comprehending God as their Father.

God set the bar for fathers. Let's look into His Word to see what He has to say about His role as our Father.

First of all, Jesus called Him "Abba Father," a term designating a close, intimate relationship. It translates "Daddy" and gives us a glimpse into the Father–Son relationship of the first two Persons of the Trinity.

But did you know that believers can also call God "Abba Father"? The Holy Spirit dwelling in us seals our adoption as sons and daughters of God (see above two verses).

Okay, enough preaching. Let's look at what a father does.

First of all, a father *provides*. Food, clothing, shelter, guidance, wisdom. God provided for the children of Israel as they trekked through the wilderness: water from rocks, manna from heaven, and when they wanted meat, quail. He guided them with the pillar of fire by night and the cloud by day. When it stopped, they stopped. When it moved, they moved.

God continues to provide for His children today. "And my God will supply every need of yours according to his riches in glory by Christ Jesus" (Philippians 4:19).

How has God provided for a specific need of yours?

Second, a father *helps*. Like my father did when my brother woke him up in the middle of the night, God will answer when we call to Him. In fact, He invites us: "Call upon me in the day of trouble; I will deliver you, and you shall glorify me" (Psalm 50:15).

How has God helped you in your day of trouble?

Third, a father *disciplines*. Discipline is not always punishment, although punishment may be part of discipline. Its purpose is to train us to live right, to strengthen us, to make us into the persons God wants us to be. "My son, do not despise the LORD's discipline and do not loathe His reproof; for the LORD disciplines those He loves, as a father the son in whom he delights (Proverbs 3:11–12).

How has God's discipline made you a better person?

And finally, a father *loves*. Sacrificially (John 3:16), unconditionally (Romans 5:8), steadfastly (Psalm 36:5), and eternally (Psalm 136:9).

When I read Zephaniah 3:17, I see God as a Father standing over the crib of His child, watching him sleep; holding him close and soothing him, softly crooning a lullaby.

You, child of God, are that child.

No matter how faithful or unfaithful our earthly fathers are, God, thank You for being the kind of father each of us needs. Amen.

MORE TEA: Read and meditate on Zephaniah 3:17.

Letter to Daddy

Dear Daddy,

I miss you. Indeed, there isn't a day that goes by that I don't think of you. Who would have imagined your little girl to be the age you were when you slipped from this life into the next?

I looked for you, you know, the night you died. I expected to come home from the hospital and find something amiss—a radio or light mysteriously turned on—to tell me your spirit had come to say one last goodbye. But no.

Not until the morning of your funeral, my twentieth birthday. Even before I opened my eyes, I felt it—a presence in me and around me—of ultimate peace, love, and joy. A velvet-like presence so real I felt I could reach out and touch it. That presence stayed with me all that day. I still get goose bumps when I think about it.

I've read about heaven—about people who have died, went there, then returned. I'm reading a book now, *I Believe in Heaven: Real Stories from the Bible, History, and Today* by Cecil Murphy and Twila Belk, that reminds me of that time—the scenarios perfectly describe the presence I was gifted with to see me through your funeral. A birthday present I'll never forget.

I remember so much about you—your thinning salt-and-pepper hair that stuck up in the morning as you mused (or snoozed?) over your coffee. I called you "Scrappy," after the cartoon character by that name. To this day I don't know why. Scrappy had more hair than you! You used to tell me that when you were young, you had wavy, blond hair, and now it was waving you goodbye.

Like a kaleidoscope, scenes with you play in my mind—spending time in your woodshop, straddling one of your sawhorses, inhaling the fragrance of freshly cut lumber. The gleaming red and white tricycle waiting for me on the sidewalk, sparkling in the morning sun, its streamers billowing in the breeze. And I thought Mom had said no.

Then there was the arrow I shot through the garage window. You just chuckled, covered up the hole with plywood, and cautioned me to be more careful.

Then those tumultuous teen years. The night you went out in your pajamas to look for me when I'd walked a friend home after a church bazaar and neglected to call you. Those were the days before cell phones, and she lived on the other side of town. By the time I climbed the front porch steps, you were so angry with me, you grounded me for a month. I understand your panic now, Dad. But between the two of us? I was glad you grounded me. I'd agreed to go out with someone I really didn't want to go out with, and the grounding gave me a good excuse to bow out without hurting the guy's feelings.

More memories surface than I have room for here. But the common denominator, Dad, was your love for me. I never doubted it for an instant, even when you told this thirteen-year-old I'd wear bobby socks until I was sixteen.

I love you, Daddy. Happy Father's Day in heaven.

Your baby girl all grown up,
Michele

MORE TEA: Read and meditate on Revelation 21:1–22:5.

My Father's Lap

In the shadow of thy wings I will take refuge, till the storms of destruction pass by. —Psalm 57:1 RSV

WHEN I WAS GROWING up, there was only one place where I could escape my mother's wrath—my father's lap. I was an impulsive child, and my mother wasn't blessed with patience, so when our wills clashed, sparks flew.

Mom was the firestorm; Dad the quiet stream. I loved them both, but it was to Dad I turned when I needed a listening ear or when I just needed cuddled. Curled up in his lap, resting my head on his shoulder, feeling his arms around me, was the safest place in the world.

Fast-forward forty years. I am now a mother, still a bit impulsive, fiery when I get going. My husband is like my father—a soothing balm to my blistering heat. One of my children has impulsively done something that could cast a dark shadow over the future. I am so furious, I shake. I feel heat radiating from my face.

"How could you do this?" I shout. "When we get home, you will tell your father what you've done."

But the scene doesn't turn out as I expect. There, curled up in my husband's lap, is our errant, remorseful child.

Fast-forward eight more years. I am now a grandmother. As my family has multiplied, so have my love and concern. I pray for my children and grandchildren every day, but still I worry. I am at the age where I realize how fragile life really is and how dangerous a place the world is. I have much more to lose now.

As I sit in the family room, my head rests on the wing of the love seat where I'm curled up. Eyes closed, I imagine myself sitting in my heavenly Father's lap, resting my head on His shoulder, feeling His arms around me.

I speak no words, but peace, like a placid stream, gently seeps into my soul. I am in the safest place in the world.

Abba Father, thank You for Your unconditional love. Amen.

MORE TEA: Read and meditate on Psalm 57.

Missing Daddy

Blessed is the man . . . –Psalm 1:1

I WROTE THE POEM sitting at a carrel in the college library, gazing out the window at the blue sky and worrying about my dad. It was the summer before he died. I attended summer sessions that year, with the plan to graduate in three years.

With every visit home, I noticed Dad getting thinner and thinner, his skin turning a grayish hue. He'd lie on his back on the hardwood floor, explaining the pain as recurrent from injuries sustained in the Battle of Attu during World War II—nearly thirty years earlier.

I had my doubts, but he assured me he'd consulted with both his personal physician and a chiropractor. Something deep inside me knew something was seriously wrong, and so, from the depths of my heart, I composed the following poem, which I slipped into his casket four months later.

I share it with you now, with the hope that its words will stir up warm memories of your own fathers. And, fathers, that you would see into the hearts of your children. Time goes by so quickly. Cherish every moment.

DAD, MY DAD

Dad, my Dad, where have you gone?
I once walked by your side.
My two small steps could never match
Your slow but gentle stride.

My small hand in yours would rest;
You were a giant then,
But yet so gentle, yet so kind—
My hero among men.

Dad, my Dad, where have you gone?
Your lap was once my throne.
Your hair, a crown of grizzled black,
To gray when I had grown.

Dad, you shouldn't work so hard—
You're getting much too thin.
Go out and shoot a round of golf;
Take me, for sure you'll win.

Father dear, I'm far away,
I need a loving hand
To slip me change when I go broke
And gently reprimand.

Dad, my Dad, where have you gone?
My son walks by my side.
His two small steps will never match
Your slow, but gentle stride.

Thank you, Lord, that even though I still miss my daddy after forty-seven years, I know I will see him in heaven. Amen.

MORE TEA: Read and meditate on Psalm 1.

The Apple of His Eye

Keep me as the apple of your eye. –Psalm 17:8 NIV

My dearest child,

You are the apple of My eye. Sometimes, I know, you feel as though I've abandoned you. I have not. I'm here. I've always been here, and I'll always be here for you. I'll never abandon you, no matter what happens, no matter how you feel or behave. No strings attached. I love you simply because you are Mine.

I'm sure you've heard the expression "the apple of my eye" many times, but do you know what it means? The "apple" of the eye is the pupil, the center of the eye and the part that allows light in. Without this delicate part, you wouldn't be able to see. So the pupil—the apple—must be protected at all costs.

I am your protector, the shield around you, the strong tower into which you may run for refuge. I am your rock, your fortress, your deliverer, your stronghold in times of trouble. Yet there have been times you haven't run to Me. You've sought help elsewhere. I never force you to come to Me. I always give you the choice.

Sometimes your choices break My heart. But I want you to love Me and choose to obey Me on your own. Like the pupil, I want you to open up your heart and allow My light and love in.

There are times when I must intervene for your own good. What parent would allow a child to step out into a busy street and not run and snatch that precious one from harm's way?

When you're weary and bearing a heavy load, I lead you to a place of rest where your soul can be refreshed. If I didn't, you'd run yourself to death. What are you trying to prove, dear one? You don't have to earn My love or prove your worth to Me. I created you. Just as you are. For a purpose. Everything I allow in your life has a purpose, child. Work *with* the circumstances, not against them. I am in control, whether you believe it or not.

Sometimes I allow hardships in your life to teach you, to strengthen you. Do you remember learning to ride a bike? How many scrapes and bruises did you endure before you were able to ride without your father running right behind you, ready to catch you if you fell?

Yet there came a time when I had to stand back and let you do it on your own. I watched you fall, brush yourself off, and hop back on again. I was so proud of you. I watched you cry when the pain was more than you could bear, when you were so frustrated because, after all your efforts, it still wasn't working out the way you'd planned. I hurt because you hurt. I counted your tears and bottled them as a reminder of your growth pains. However, I was always there.

As you grew, the lessons became harder. Such is life, My child. Sometimes I allowed you to wander in a wilderness, to struggle in a storm. It pained me to hear you cry, "Where are You? Why don't You help me?" I *was* helping you. I never abandoned you. Your faith had to grow stronger, and the wilderness and storms make perfect faith-growing greenhouses.

You, the apple of My eye, are precious to Me, and I love you so much. There isn't anything I wouldn't give for you. Indeed, I gave My Son.

You are the apple of My eye. Don't ever forget it.

Love,

Abba Father

MORE TEA: Read and meditate on Zephaniah 3:17.

Labor Day

Whatever you do, work at it with all your heart, as working for the Lord, not for men.

–Colossians 3:23 NIV

A Better Life

Whatever you do, work at it with all your heart, as working for the Lord, not for men. –Colossians 3:23 NIV

ON APRIL 26, 1910, my grandmother, Anna Bortnik, boarded the *Kaiser Wilhelm II* in Bremen, Germany, after traveling across Europe from her native village of Lenarts, Hungary. Nine days later she arrived in New York. She was seventeen years old. The only language she knew was Slovak.

In the early 1900s America was the place to be. Like my grandmother, they came from all over Europe, bringing their work ethic to steel mills, coal mines, factories, and farms. No job was too menial—to them it was an opportunity to make a better life for themselves and their families.

My grandmother found employment in a sewing factory in New Jersey until she married a steel mill worker. Mike Demchak, a widower, took her home to a ready-made family in the Monongahela Valley near Pittsburgh. There she raised nine children alone after Mike died of pneumonia in 1934, while the country was in the throes of the Great Depression. One by one, her children dropped out of school to support the family, while she took in washing and ironing.

I once asked my mother how they survived the Depression.

"We were so poor we didn't even know there *was* a Depression," she said.

By today's standards, my grandmother had a hard life. Yet I never heard her complain. From her perspective, what was there to complain about? She had a roof over her head, food in the pantry, and clothes enough for every season.

For the most part, my grandparents' generation, through their hard work, succeeded in making better lives for themselves and their children. In the process, they created a better world.

Work gives our lives purpose and meaning. Even in perfect Eden, Adam and Eve had a job to do: "The LORD God took the man and put him in the Garden of Eden to work it and take care of it" (Genesis 2:15).

Too often, though, we see work as drudgery, something that must be endured for us to survive. We feel like the ditch digger, caught in a deadening, joy-stealing cycle: "I digga the ditch to make the money to buy the food to give me the strength to digga the ditch."

But work was meant to be enjoyable and rewarding: "Then I realized it is good and proper for a man to eat and drink, and find satisfaction in his toilsome labor . . . to accept his lot and be happy in his work," Solomon wrote (Ecclesiastes 5:18–19).

The fruit of our labor is ours to enjoy: "You will eat the fruit of your labor" (Psalm 128:2).

Let not Labor Day be only a day that marks the end of the summer season and the start of the new school year. Let it be what it was created to be: a tribute to the workers of America and a celebration of their achievements. For hard work is what made this country great, and hard work is what will keep it great.

Father, bless the workers of this nation. May they find in their jobs fulfillment of the purpose You have for each one. Amen.

MORE TEA: Read and meditate on Ecclesiastes 5:18–20; Ephesians 6:5–9.

NOTE: I obtained important information about my grandmother from the ship's manifest, which I was able to view online on the Ellis Island Website: www.ellisisland.org/

While researching my grandmother's journey, I discovered that the country of Czechoslovakia wasn't established until 1918—eight years after she immigrated to the US. Although my grandmother had lived in Hungary, her ethnic background was Slovak.

Why Do I Work?

In My Father's house are many mansions. . . . I go to prepare a place for you. –John 14:2 NKJV

Don't store up treasures here on earth. . . . store them in heaven where they will never lose their value, and are safe from thieves. – Matthew 6:19–20 LB

IN HIS SHORT STORY "The Mansion," Henry Van Dyke tells of John Weightman, a highly successful, self-made businessman whose life was ruled by one motto: "Nothing that does not bring the reward."

Weightman applied this motto to both his professional and personal life, from investing his money to building his richly furnished house to raising his children to giving to charity. A faithful churchgoer and professed Christian, Weightman believed that Scripture promised a reward for good deeds.

Weightman even had a carefully crafted career plan for his son, Harold, who, unbeknownst to Weightman, chafed under his father's iron hand. One Christmas Eve Harold asked his father to help an ill friend who'd saved the young man from going the wrong way in his early college years. Harold suggested they loan him three or four thousand dollars.

When Weightman was told the young man had only "a fighting chance," he balked.

"A fighting chance may do for a speculation, but it is not a good investment," he said. "Send him three or four hundred dollars."

That night, feeling sad after the disagreement with Harold, Weightman fell asleep in his carved library chair. He dreamed he died and went to heaven, where people, all of less fortune and prosperity than himself, told him they were on their way to their mansions. Surely, Weightman thought, with all the good he'd done, his mansion would far outdo anyone else's. And he felt a certain smug pleasure imagining their reactions to his place.

One by one, each of his fellow travelers was escorted to mansions so beautiful they were filled with joy and awe. Finally only Weightman and his friend Dr. Mclean were left. The heavenly guide led them to one of the largest and fairest mansions with a spectacular flower garden. The guide turned to the doctor.

"This is for you," he said. "All the good that you have done for others, all the help that you have given, all the comfort that you have brought, all the strength and love that you have bestowed upon the suffering, are here; for we have built them all into this mansion for you."

Now it was Weightman's turn. He could hardly wait. The guide led him to a single, ramshackle hut in an open, lonely field with no flowers and very little grass. It looked like it had been built with scraps and castoffs of other buildings. Surely this was a mistake!

The guide shook his head sadly. "This is all the material you sent us," he explained.

"All my life long I have been doing things that must have supplied you with material," Weightman said. "I have built a schoolhouse; the wing of a hospital; two—yes, three—small churches, and the greater part of a large one, the spire of St. Petro—"

"Yes," answered the Keeper of the Gate, "it counts in the world—where you counted it. But it does not belong to you here. We have saved and used everything that you sent us. This is the mansion prepared for you."

I wonder—what are *my* motives for the things I do? I listed all the possible reasons I could have for serving God. Love for Him was at the top of the list—the purest and hardest one of all. I would like to think I serve because I love Him. I would like to think that is my only reason.

But I also work for that heavenly reward—that mansion Scripture promises.

I confess I'm a lot like Weightman. I long for earthly recognition, appreciation, approval, worldly goods, health, a good life, popularity, achieving my dreams. Would I still serve Him if I were to attain none of these?

I would like to think I would, but I know I still have a way to go to have the pure heart God wants me to have.

Dear God, help me to keep my eyes fixed on You, not on what I could get for being obedient. Help me to give and to serve for pure reasons—to want to help someone else with no thought of myself. Amen.

MORE TEA: Read and meditate on 1 Corinthians 3:10–15; Matthew 6:1–4, 19–21.

Thanksgiving

Give thanks to the LORD, for he is good.

–Psalm 118:1 NIV

Only Temporary

*I have learned to get along happily whether I have much or little. –
Philippians 4:11 NLT*

THIRTY-EIGHT YEARS AGO, we moved into an unfinished
basement fifteen miles from town, hoping to save rent money
as we built our house ourselves. I was a stay-at-home mom, so
money was scarce with just my husband's income—and even
that was sometimes only a hundred dollars a week.

The children were still toddlers—Todd was four, and Jaime
was 11 months—and boxes, clothes, and toys cluttered every
square foot as I struggled to make that concrete cubicle a home.
The furnace, on loan from my husband's boss until we could
afford a new one (which ended up being twenty-five years later), needed repair. It was already mid-November, and winter
was closing in fast. A constant fire in the woodstove did little to
warm up the concrete surrounding us. Insulating the place was
still on our "to do" list. I wore long underwear, a toboggan hat,
and layers of clothing indoors.

The plumbing was unfinished, so we hooked up a garden
hose to the water tank and fed it through the hole in the wall
above the tub meant for the fixtures. Lugging pots of hot water

from the kitchen, I'd flooded the floor twice getting the kids' bath ready.

My back ached from sleeping on an old, lumpy sofa bed mattress so thin I could feel the support bars. Our comfortable queen-size bed was still in the wagon shed, where we temporarily stored items while we unpacked and organized.

Three days of disorganization, interruptions, and things gone wrong left perfectionist me struggling with my emotions. *Why can't I have nice things, the easy way, like everyone else?* I wondered. *Why am I always a "have not" and never a "have"?*

Although I tried not to complain (too much), my husband knew I was struggling and tried to cheer me up. "It's only temporary," he'd say when my impatience oozed through the growing cracks in my composure.

"Yeah, right," I'd answer.

Then an early snowstorm dumped six inches on the countryside overnight. Every two hours I bundled up even more and shoveled swirling drifts away from the only door. Flinging heavy, wet snow over my shoulder, I finally gave in to self-pity.

"Temporary, temporary," I fumed. "Is *everything* temporary?"

The answer came immediately. *Even if you had everything exactly the way you wanted, it would still be temporary.*

I couldn't argue with that.

Lord, help me to remember that my earthly condition, whether rich, poor, or in-between, is only temporary. Remind me daily what's really important. Amen.

MORE TEA: Read and meditate on 1 Timothy 6:6–8.

Starfish Saver or Scrooge?

He who is kind to the poor lends to the LORD, and he will reward him for what he has done. –Proverbs 19:17 NIV

WHEN THE AMERICAN MISSIONARY asked Volodia what he wanted most, the twelve-year-old Russian boy answered, "A normal life."

Volodia is one of an estimated 55,000 homeless children who live on the streets and in the sewers of St. Petersburg, Russia, because their parents are either drunkards or too poor to keep them, or both. These children have little trust in adults, for the very people entrusted with their care have abused them.

An orphanage is not the answer to the problem, either, because the conditions in post-Communist Russia are deplorable. These children feel safer living in the streets or under the city, although disease, starvation, and exposure claim many before they have the chance to grow up.

There was a time when I wanted to help everyone whose story touched my heart, like this one did. I was a softy. But the more pleas I heard, the more frustrated and confused I became. I couldn't help everyone.

Not only was I overwhelmed, but in time I became afflicted with the-more-I-have-the-more-it-has-me syndrome. I wanted to cling to my blessings, justifying my selfishness by reminding myself that for so long I had so little. I became a Scrooge.

God has been nudging me of late, placing in front of me opportunities to give of my abundance, through Samaritan's Purse (Christmas Shoeboxes for Children), Compassion International, and Micaiah Ministries. I've had the chance to aid hurricane victims in America, earthquake victims in Asia, and children in a Haitian orphanage, as well as send care packages to soldiers in Iraq.

I'm sad to say I haven't made the most of these opportunities. "I'm too busy" and "I give in my own way" are flimsy excuses. I have so much. They have so little.

But others are finding ways to help. Micaiah Ministries, for example, is working to give these Russian children the normal life they so desperately want. It has purchased a house in St. Petersburg for fifteen of these children. They will finally have a mother.

When there are 55,000 homeless children, how can this make a difference?

It's like the story of the little boy who took an early morning walk along the beach, where the tide had left thousands of starfish stranded. As he walked along, the boy bent down, picked up a starfish and gently tossed it back into the ocean. An older man walking behind him asked him what he was doing.

"The sun is up, and the tide is going out," the boy answered. "If I don't throw them in, they'll die."

"But, young man," the older man pointed out, "don't you realize that there are miles and miles of beach and starfish all along it? You can't possibly make a difference!"

The boy bent down, scooped up another starfish and tossed it into the ocean. Turning to the man, he said, "It made a difference for that one."

God doesn't ask us to do it all, to give to every organization that pleads for our help. But He does ask us to do our part.

During this season of Thanksgiving, let us not only express gratitude for the many blessings we have—and often take for granted—let us share our abundance with those who have so much less. Our combined efforts will impact the world in a way we can't even imagine, if we each made a difference for just one little starfish.

Lord, my cup is overflowing. Let not the excess go to waste. Show me how use it to help others and spread your blessings around. Help me to be a softy once again. Amen.

MORE TEA: Read and meditate on Matthew 25:31–40.

Thanksliving

His compassions never fail. They are new every morning; great is your faithfulness. —Lamentations 3:23 NIV

THANKSGIVING—THE WORD CONJURES up visions of turkey with all the trimmings, pumpkin pie, family get-togethers, and deer season. It's time to set the candles in the window, hang the holly, hit the malls, and hide the bathroom scale. For the next month or so, we'll be eating, shopping, baking, cleaning, decorating, visiting, and partying. We'll go from "thanks" to "giving" to "living" as life reaches its peak December 25 and settles down after January 1.

Recently, as I reflected on what God has done for me this past year, I took the word "thanksgiving" and, using the letters, listed things for which I am grateful:

T—I'm thankful for my trials, for they send me to my knees, reminding me of how much I need God. A wise Christian once wrote that our trials are tailor-made: "Your Lord hath the choice of ten thousand other crosses, to exercise you withal; but His wisdom and His love choose out this for you, beside them all. Take it as a choice one, and make use of it" (Samuel Rutherford).

H—I'm thankful for my husband, who is a true helpmeet. I'm thankful for my house, my home, my health, hugs, heaven, hope, my hands, my hair, my hearing. I'm thankful for the Holy Spirit, who guides, comforts, and teaches me.

A—I'm thankful for Almighty God, El-Shaddai, Adonai, Abba Father, the Alpha and the Omega. I'm thankful for not only abundance and abilities, but also my aches and afflictions. I'm thankful for angels, "ministering spirits sent to serve those who will inherit salvation" (Hebrews 1:14). I'm thankful I'm alive.

N—I'm thankful for the night, for in it I cease from my labors and rest. I'm thankful for the dark night of the soul, for as I wrestle though it, I know that dawn, and light, will come, and my strivings will make me stronger.

K—I'm thankful for kisses, kids, and kindness.

S—I'm thankful for strength for the day, a strength not my own that sees me through. I'm thankful for second chances, the sun, and the Son. And I'm thankful that we finally have siding on our house.

G—I'm thankful for grace, for all the wonderful blessings I have that I have not earned, that I don't deserve.

I—I'm thankful for Immanuel, "God with us"—that God sent His Son from the glory of heaven to the bowels of earth to show me what He is like. I'm thankful for having the best insurance policy around, for when life comes at me fast and furious, I have more than an insurance company on my side. I have God Himself.

V—I'm thankful for the victory won on Calvary's cross, so my sins, "like scarlet, shall be as white as snow" (Isaiah 1:18) and are removed from me "as far as the east is from the west" (Psalm 103:12).

I—I'm thankful for the intercession of others and for the integrity I see in people around me.

N—I'm thankful for new things, especially new birth (John 3:16), new life (1 John 5:11–12), a new song ((Psalm 40:3), and a new me (2 Corinthians 5:17).

G—I'm thankful for grandchildren, gifts, generosity, guidance, Golgotha, and the Goliaths I face.

The list could go on, but I've used up my allotted space. Isn't it great to have more blessings than the space in which to list them?

Dear readers, I challenge you: from now until Thanksgiving Day, why not take a letter a day, and list all the things for which you are thankful? You'll find, as I did, that God's compassions are new every morning. Great is His faithfulness!

Thank You, God, for all that You are to me and all that You do in my life. Amen.

MORE TEA: Read and meditate on Psalm 103.

Thanksgiving Thoughts

For the LORD is good and his love endures forever; his faithfulness continues through all generations. –Psalm 100:5 NIV

GOD HAS GIVEN ME many gifts. In this season of Thanksgiving, I'm going to dwell on three of them: the past, the present, and the future.

I'm thankful for my past, especially that I grew up in a home where I witnessed my mother talking to God all day long. "Don't You let it rain," she'd say when she hung the laundry on the line. I'm sure that's why I still live with an awareness of God's *abiding presence* moment by moment.

"Where can I go from your Spirit? Where can I flee from your presence? If I go up to the heavens, you are there; if I make my bed in the depths, you are there. If I rise on the wings of the dawn, if I settle on the far side of the sea, even there your hand will guide me, your right hand will hold me fast" (Psalm 139:7–10 NIV).

Which brings me to the second gift for which I'm thankful: the present. For the freezer and panty shelves stocked with the vegetables we harvested from our garden. For the firewood stacked in the barn. For health and energy. For Friday night date nights with my husband. For our nine beautiful, fun grandchildren. For my husband's job. For opportunities to work out of my home doing what I love best. For the sunsets and sunrises and birds and trees and butterflies and all God created for our enjoyment and use. God's *abundant provision* blows me away.

"Do not be anxious about anything, but in everything by prayer and petition, with thanksgiving, present your requests to God . . . And my God will meet all your needs according to his glorious riches" (Philippians 4:6, 19 NIV).

Glory . . . that brings me to the third thing for which I'm thankful: the future.

There's quite a bit of interest these days in end times. Some believed 2012 would be the last year for planet Earth. I wasn't too worried about it. I don't put a whole lot of stock in man's predictions. My Bible tells me only God knows when this will be. So why get all stressed about it?

Besides, whether the world ends this year or after, I know where I'll spend eternity: heaven (1 John 5:11–12). In the meantime, I know that God has a plan and purpose for me (Psalm 138:8). Watching God's *awesome plan* for my life as it unfolds day by day is more exciting than the latest special effects movie.

"For I know the plans I have for you," declares the LORD, "plans to prosper you and not to harm you, plans to give you hope and a future" (Jeremiah 29:11 NIV).

"The one thing I do, however, is to forget what is behind me and do my best to reach what is ahead. So I run straight toward the goal in order to win the prize, which is God's call through Christ Jesus to the life above" (Philippians 3:13–14 TEV).

Past, present, future—my times are in His hand (Psalm 31:15).

Thank you, Lord, for Your abiding presence, abundant provision, and awesome plan. Amen.

MORE TEA: Read and meditate on Joel 2:23–24;
Habakkuk 3:17–18.

Thanksgiving—Then and Now

For I have learned, in whatsoever state I am, therewith to be content. –Philippians 4:11 KJV

I'm thankful for the muddy floor
that greets me every day.
I'm thankful for the dirty socks
that on the floor doth lay.
I'm thankful for the fingerprints
that deck both chair and wall.
I'm thankful for the daily dust
that on the desk doth fall.
I'm thankful for my kitchen sink
that hides the dirty dish.
I'm thankful for the splattered wall
from when I fried the fish.
I'm thankful for the Cheerios,
Play-Doh, and other yuck,
And all the stones and crayons
that plug my sweeper up.

I'm thankful for the toothpaste
smeared on the bathroom door.
I'm thankful for the wad of gum
stuck to the kitchen floor.
I'm thankful for the scattered toys
that often pierce my feet
When I must run to get the phone
before I've time to sweep.
I'm thankful for the mending
I love so much to do
That I hide it in the corner
and buy them something new.
I'm thankful for the unmade beds
—they mean I'm not alone.
I'm thankful for so many things
that make our house a home.

I wrote the above poem years ago when the kids were still home and driving me crazy. Oh, how I longed for the time they'd be all grown up and on their own! Oh, how I craved a house that stayed clean and "redd up."

Now the kids are grown and gone, raising families of their own. The house stays clean—and too quiet. I miss the noise and chaos that come with raising a family.

Can't we humans ever be happy? When we have one thing, we yearn for something else. When we have that something else, we want what we had.

Why, I wonder, can't I be like the Apostle Paul, who said he was content whatever the circumstances of life (Philippians 4:11)? And he wrote those words while under house arrest. I felt like I was under house arrest back when I wrote that poem.

But time moves on, doesn't it?

I'm learning to embrace each season of my life as it unfolds, whether or not it unfolds the way I'd planned and dreamed.

You see, God is in control, and He has a purpose for each of us in every season of life. He knows the end from the beginning. "All the days ordained for me were written in Your book before one of them came to be," the psalmist wrote (Psalm 139:16).

This year we'll celebrate Thanksgiving the Saturday following the holiday. Our oldest son, who loves to cook, will prepare a turkey dinner. Our youngest son and his girlfriend will drive home from Ebensburg for the day. Three of our grandchildren will be here. Sometime during the chaos, our daughter, who lives 650 miles away, will call and the phone will be passed around.

The house will ring with laughter and conversation and family love—and remind me that my house is still a home.

You have blessed me with so much, Lord. Remind me in my disgruntled moments to be content with whatever I have—because whatever I have comes from You, the giver of every perfect gift (James 1:17). Amen.

MORE TEA: Read and meditate on Philippians 4:4–13.

The Boxes on the Porch

As a matter of equality your abundance at the present time should supply their want, so that their abundance may supply your want. –2 *Corinthians 8:14 RSV*

IT WAS DURING OUR poor years that God taught me the formula for giving and receiving. God's lessons, I find, often come when circumstances are lowest and there seems to be no way out, when I feel as though I'm at the bottom of a deep hole and someone throws in a shovel.

The incident I am about to relate was during one of those "deep hole" times.

When I had my first child, I chose to be a stay-at-home mom and resigned from my full-time teaching job, giving up all that came with it—a healthy paycheck, benefits, seniority, job security. Although I knew it would be difficult financially, I believed that if we were doing the right thing, God would provide. I was clueless as to exactly how difficult it would really be.

After trying to live on one income that often provided a meager $100 a week for a family of three, my husband and I were exploring alternate sources of income that would allow me to stay home. At the time we were attempting to build a retail business that involved both selling product and recruiting others to sell.

Our cupboards were bare—literally. Our son ate "ketchup bread" (ketchup smeared sparingly on a slice of bread) as a snack. Peanut butter and jelly were luxuries we couldn't afford. Meatless meals were standard fare, and chicken soup was on the menu more often than my husband cared for.

One Saturday evening the phone rang.

"You left something on your porch," a voice told me before the line went dead.

I looked at my husband, puzzled.

"Did you leave anything on the porch?" I asked him.

"I don't think so," he responded.

We went downstairs—we had a second floor apartment at the time—and there on the porch were three boxes of food! Among the cans and boxes were several packages of meat. Oh, blessed meat! I wanted to cry. I felt happy, relieved, grateful, and humbled.

That night was a turning point. We vowed that we would someday be in a position to help others. The following spring we planted a vegetable garden. I picked berries and learned to can and preserve food. Babysitting supplemented my husband's income while allowing me to stay home with my son. Circumstances gradually improved. My husband eventually got a better-paying job. When the kids started school, I began to substitute teach.

Our three children are all grown and gone now, and we're in the position to be the givers. It's a wonderful place to be, but I've learned that it's just as important to be good receivers, too, accepting with humility and gratitude what is given in love.

We never found out who put the boxes on the porch that night, but they left us with more than a gift of food. They gave us hope and the desire to do for others what had been done for us.

And that's a gift money can't buy.

Thank you, Lord, that I was needy and "less fortunate" because through my need You taught me how to give. Amen.

MORE TEA: Read and meditate on 2 Corinthians 8:1–15.

The Thanksgiving Cemetery Run

Remember the days of old; consider generations long past.
–Deuteronomy 32:7 NIV

OUR THANKSGIVING TRADITIONS ARE, once again, changing, and not of our own doing or choice.

Growing up, my husband and I had different Thanksgiving traditions. While he spent the day with a whole clan of relatives, enjoying Grandma's pies—and she baked plenty and a variety—I spent the day quietly reading while my mother, who shooed everyone out of the kitchen, prepared a turkey dinner for just the five of us. If any relative stopped in, it was for only a few minutes. We certainly never went anywhere on Thanksgiving Day.

Fast-forward twenty years. Now married with my own family, I wanted to begin a new tradition: we hosted Thanksgiving dinner and invited Dean's parents, and his sister and her family.

By then my own family was scattered. My brother and sister, both out-of-state, had established their own Thanksgiving traditions. My father had passed away, and my mother was grappling with Alzheimer's disease.

This tradition ran its cycle until our three children grew up. I never wanted them to feel obligated to come home for the holidays but rather to establish their own traditions. After all, isn't that what we raise them for? To live their own lives, to make their own mark in their corner of the world.

But we still celebrated the day with some of our ever-growing family. I didn't have to cook the entire meal any longer—just bring a dish or two—and that was just fine by me.

Then life changed. Again. One year we faced spending the day by ourselves. I realize there are those for whom Thanksgiving (and any other holiday) is "just another day." But we didn't want it to be that way for us. We have too many good memories of Thanksgiving past.

So my husband suggested something unusual: take the day and visit the cemeteries where our parents and grandparents are buried—to thank them for what they contributed to our lives.

And with our oldest son accompanying us, that's what we did. On Thanksgiving Day, we drove 246 miles, stopped at six cemeteries, and visited our forebears—Dean's parents and grandparents, buried in Jefferson County, Pennsylvania, and my parents and godparents in the Mon Valley (near Donora, Pennsylvania). We reminisced—even our son had memories of these precious folks, even though I'd thought he was too young to remember.

We drove through two cemeteries where my grandparents are buried. I didn't know exactly where their graves were, but just driving through was like a trip down memory lane, my mind and heart making connections I'd avoided making for far too long.

No, it wasn't morbid. It was enlightening. And freeing.

Connecting with our past, touching base with our heritage, we realized how truly blessed we are. We are what we are because of what they were and what they did.

Seeing those gravestones gave us not a sense of loss or finality but of continuity and hope. We are, we realized, the connection between the past and the future.

"We should note the days of old. They are what mold us" (Curt Lovelace, "Memorializing the Past, A Practice in Remembering God's Goodness").

Who knows? Maybe we started a new tradition: The Thanksgiving Cemetery Run.

Thank you, Father God, for reminding us of the rich heritage we have. Help us to pass along that legacy to our children and grandchildren. May they, too, comprehend the continuity of life. Amen.

MORE TEA: Read and meditate on Joshua 4:1–7.

The Well, the Ram, and Jehovah Jireh

And then God opened her eyes and she saw a well of water. – *Genesis 21:19 NIV*

Abraham looked up and . . . saw a ram. –Genesis 22:13 NIV

I'VE ALWAYS FELT THAT Hagar, Sarah's Egyptian maidservant, got a raw deal. Her job was to serve her mistress. This she did. And what did it get her? Not five gold stars for obedience, that's for sure.

We first meet her in the pages of ancient Scripture when barren Sarah decides the only way she'll have children is to order her maidservant to sleep with her husband. Any child conceived as a result would then be considered Sarah's. Legally.

So Hagar sleeps with the big man and conceives. Sarah's abuse of her pregnant maidservant is so harsh Hagar runs away. But God meets her in the wilderness, gives her a blessing, and sends her back. Fast-forward about fifteen years to the weaning celebration of Abraham and Sarah's miracle baby, Isaac. Sarah spots half-brother Ishmael taunting the little guy and runs to Abraham. "Get rid of that slave woman and her son!" she orders him.

The next morning, Abraham gives Hagar some food and water and sends her off into the wilderness.

When the water was gone, she put Ishmael under a bush and went off a short distance, where she sat sobbing, "I cannot watch him die."

Once again God meets her in the wilderness. I love how the writer of Genesis describes what happens next: "God heard the boy crying" (Genesis 21:17) and "God opened her eyes and she saw a well of water" (v. 19).

They do not die in the wilderness. Ishmael becomes "a great nation," as God promised his mother.

Fast-forward again, this time to Abraham and Isaac on a mountain on the land of Moriah, where God has sent Abraham on a mission: "Take your son, your only son, Isaac, and . . . sacrifice him there as a burnt offering" (Genesis 22:2).

They were almost there when Isaac asks, "Where is the lamb for the burnt offering?"

I used to wonder if Abraham's answer, "God himself will provide the lamb," was a cop-out. I mean, would he really tell Isaac *he* was the offering? And I used to think Abraham lied when he told the servants to wait at the bottom of the mountain: "I and the boy will go over there. We will worship and then *we* will come back to you" (Genesis 22:5, emphasis mine).

Then on the mountain, just after God has stayed his hand from plunging the sacrificial knife into Isaac's heart, "Abraham looked up and . . . saw a ram," which he sacrificed in place of Isaac.

Did the ram just happen to be there? Or had it been there all along, making its way up the mountain and getting itself stuck in the thicket just as Abraham looked up?

Did the well that provided life-giving water to Hagar and Ishmael just happen to be there? Some commentators say it was there all along, but Hagar, in her physical, emotional, mental, and spiritual condition, just didn't see it. Some say it was well hidden.

The answer to these questions is the name that Abraham gives to the mountain: "The-LORD-Will-Provide"(YHWH Yireh or Jehovah Jireh).

The Hebrew word used for "provide" also means "to see."

God is still Jehovah Jireh today.

Thank you, Lord, for reminding me of the value of every person on this planet. "For God so loved the world, that He gave His only Son" (John 3:16). Amen.

MORE TEA: Read and meditate on Genesis 21:14–21; 22:1–19.

Advent

Prepare the way for the Lord, make straight paths for him.

–Matthew 3:3 NIV

Ready for Christmas?

Prepare the way for the LORD. *—Matthew 3:3 NIV*

ARE YOU READY FOR Christmas? That's a question we hear frequently this time of the year. What's your answer? Yes, no, almost, not even close?

Holiday preparations can be overwhelming. Just looking at my to-do list tires me out! Shop 'til I drop? Well, I drop in two hours. Spend the day cleaning, and the place looks great—but for how long? Vacuuming hurts my back. And baking? Well, in addition to the mess I have to clean up, all those carbs and calories send my blood sugar skyrocketing and my energy level plummeting. And the cost of postage makes me think twice about mailing Christmas cards.

It was fun when the kids were around, but when they grew up and left, Christmas became not a celebration, but an unwelcome interruption in my busy schedule. How did I get so out of touch with Christmas?

I focused on the wrong thing. I worked on making a good Christmas for my children, but when they left, my Christmas spirit went right out the door with them.

To regain the true focus of Christmas, I need to remind myself that the garlands, goodies, greetings, and guests are all part of the celebration of an awesome event: God becoming flesh, fulfilling of the prophecy that "a virgin shall be with child, and shall bear a Son, and they shall call His name 'Immanuel,' which is translated 'God with us'" (Matthew 1:23; Isaiah 7:14).

To get back in touch with Christmas, I must sift through the wrappings to find the real gift—the first Christmas present ever given: the baby Immanuel: "For God so loved the world that He gave His only begotten Son, that whoever believes in Him should not perish but have everlasting life" (John 3:16).

And that's a gift worth celebrating—and a celebration worth getting ready for!

Are you ready for Christmas?

Restore my Christmas spirit, O God. Remind me of why I celebrate. Amen.

MORE TEA: Read and meditate on Isaiah 40:3–5; John 1:1–18; Colossians 1:15–19.

An Age-Old Problem
First Sunday of Advent

All have sinned and fall short of the glory of God. –Romans 3:23 NIV

SOMEWHERE BENEATH ALL THAT mud and grease was my first-born. I cringed. I didn't want him even to set foot in my clean house. When he was younger and showed up at the door looking like the mud monster of Smithport, I'd make him strip down to his underwear on the porch before I let him in. My house is *my* domain, and I alone determine who comes in and under what conditions.

Getting to heaven, God's home, isn't any different. So why do we think we can get there on our own terms and ignore God's? I once thought that if my good deeds outweighed my bad ones, if I did everything my religion told me I had to do, or if I managed to keep from doing wrong, I'd get into heaven.

The problem is, no matter how hard I try to be good, I somehow manage to do something I know displeases God. Sometimes I choose to do wrong on the spur of the moment, like the time in high school when I cheated on a history quiz.

Other times I sin without even thinking, like when I swore at the dog after I tripped over him and crashed into the cupboard. Excuses such as "It's not my fault" or "I couldn't help it" just don't wash with a holy God who cannot even look at sin.

On my own, I cannot be good enough to get into heaven. I can do nothing to remove the sin that too frequently stains my soul. Only a perfect sacrifice can do that (Hebrews 9:22). Jesus, God's Son, was that perfect sacrifice. That's why He came—to make me clean enough to enter heaven and solve that old sin problem once and for all.

Dear God, as I light the first candle on my Advent wreath, I am reminded once again of why You sent Your Son to earth: to die so that I might live forever with You in heaven. Throughout this busy holiday season, help me not to forget it. Amen.

MORE TEA: Read and meditate on Genesis 3:1–19.

The Promise
Second Sunday of Advent

A shoot will come from the stump of Jesse; from his roots a Branch will bear fruit. –Isaiah 11:1 NIV

"BEARS EXTRA-LARGE, EXTRA-SWEET, extra-firm fruit so you enjoy fresh peach flavor . . ." My mouth was watering already as I ordered two three-foot trees. It would take years of cultivation before that promise could be fulfilled, but never mind: Maybe by the time I had grandchildren, those luscious peaches would be mine.

But it was not to be. The trees never made it past the first year. I thought all hope was lost until one spring day two years later I noticed a small shoot pushing its way up through the grass. The peach tree! It wasn't dead, after all! Somehow this little branch, defying all odds, sprang up from roots I'd thought were dead.

Likewise, when all seemed hopeless for God's chosen people, the Israelites, in the darkest night of exile and oppression, He reminded them that He had not deserted them. Even as their homes, their temple, their holy city Jerusalem lay in ruins, God promised someday He would send a Savior to bring hope in the midst of despair, life in the valley of death, and healing to broken hearts and wounded spirits (Isaiah 61:1).

Sometimes the struggles of life get me down. Just when hope seems dead, God reminds me that, just as He was there for the Israelites so long ago, He's there for me today, even when I can't sense His presence. Grasping onto that tiny root of hope is all I need to get me through life's rockiest ground.

Father God, as I light the second Advent candle, I remember the dark nights of my life, when I thought all was lost. Thank you for giving me hope when I had none left. Amen.

MORE TEA: Read and meditate on Isaiah 9:2–7.

A Him-Possible Situation
Third Sunday of Advent

The virgin will be with child and will give birth to a son, and will call him Immanuel. –Isaiah 7:14 NIV

"DID IT ACTUALLY HAPPEN, or was it all a dream?" Mary wondered, stuffing an extra robe into the basket. Was Elizabeth really pregnant as the messenger had claimed?

"In her old age?" Mary almost scoffed. "Impossible!"

But then he'd added, "Nothing is impossible with God."

This impromptu trip to Jerusalem would clear up any doubts. Then she'd deal with Joseph. She couldn't imagine what his reaction would be. She already planned what she'd say.

"Joseph, I'm going to have a baby, but don't worry, I haven't been unfaithful. God sent an angel to tell me that I'm to be the mother of the Messiah we've been waiting for so long!"

Oh, brother, what a mess! Joseph was understanding, more so than most men, but even he'd laugh at something like that.

"Oh, Joseph," she sighed, remembering when he first asked her father for her hand in marriage. How she rejoiced when he'd given his consent! The dowry paid, she waited, trying to be patient, while Joseph prepared the home they would soon share. And now this.

"Joseph," she pleaded silently, "please believe me."

The angel's words echoed in her mind and sank down into her heart: *nothing is impossible with God.*

"Yes, that's it!" she thought, pulling on the lid of the basket with a flourish and fastening it to the sides. She'd leave the matter with Him.

Like Mary, I, too, often face times when I'm up against it with no way out. That's when I turn things over to God. What's impossible for me is possible for Him.

As I light the third candle on my Advent wreath, Father, I am reminded that You are still the God of the impossible. Give me Mary's simple faith when the winds of doubt blow. Amen.

MORE TEA: Read and meditate on Luke 1:26–38.

Joseph's Dilemma
Fourth Sunday of Advent

Your throne will be established forever. –2 Samuel 7:16 NIV

HE JOLTED AWAKE, HIS body drenched in sweat. The fragrance of freshly cut wood wafted through the darkness from the shop next door.

Joseph, son of David. A fancy title for a poor carpenter from Nazareth.

Don't be afraid to take Mary home as your wife, for what is conceived in her is from the Holy Spirit.

He grew up with the Scriptures. He knew the prophecies. Someday God would send Israel a Savior. But here? Now? In *his* family? What did he have to offer God? He wasn't rich, famous, or powerful, and had no influence with those who were.

She will give birth to a son, and you are to give him the name Jesus.

Jesus—one who saves. Surely the Messiah would be born in a family who had more than he. Why, it was all he could do to prepare a home for Mary. He'd worked so hard, was almost done when she shattered him with the news that she was pregnant.

"No!" he cried into the darkness. "It can't be! Not Mary!"

He knew the laws, the punishment for adultery. He had no choice. He had to do what was right. Maybe he could divorce her quietly, save them both the shame, the explanations to prying questions.

Don't be afraid to take Mary home as your wife.

Could it be? Could it really be? Joseph sat up, the fingers of dawn reaching into the shadows of his heart.

Don't be afraid.

His sense of justice gave way to the need to believe the impossible. He reached for his robe and sandals. There was much to do. Mary was waiting.

As I light the fourth candle on my Advent wreath, I pray for the strength to respond to Your call, dear God, even when I don't understand. Amen.

MORE TEA: Read and meditate on Matthew 1:18–25.

Mysterious Magi
First Sunday of Advent

At the name of Jesus every knee should bow, in heaven and on earth and under the earth, and every tongue confess that Jesus Christ is Lord, to the glory of God the Father. –Philippians 2:10–11 NIV

WHO WERE THESE DUSTY travelers who asked King Herod, "Where is the one who has been born king of the Jews?" They said they'd seen his star in the east and had traveled to Judea to worship him.

Evolved from an ancient priestly caste who studied astrology, the interpretation of dreams, natural science, and medicine, the biblical Magi were educated men who served as advisors to kings—hence their easy access to King Herod.

Centuries before, the Jewish prophet Daniel rose from an exile to a prince and chief among them, so they were familiar with his prophecies about the coming of a great king who was to rise among the Jews. When a brilliant new star appeared in the heavens, they knew the time had come to find this Promised One.

But when they got to Jerusalem, no one seemed to know anything about this "King of the Jews," not even the Jewish authorities. No one had taken the shepherds seriously when they ran through Bethlehem the night the Promised One was born, telling everyone they met they'd seen the Messiah.

Reactions to this newborn King were varied. Poor shepherds praised God for the privilege of kneeling before Him. Pagan wise men traveled thousands of miles to honor Him. Jewish authorities only five miles away ignored Him. Jealous Herod tried to kill Him.

Two thousand years later people are still divided as to what they believe about Jesus Christ. Yet the Bible says that *every* knee will bow and *every* tongue will acknowledge that He is, indeed, Lord.

Let me never, O Lord, take lightly the birth of the King of kings, Lord of lords, and Savior of the world. Amen.

MORE TEA: Read and meditate on Matthew 2:1–12.

Titles
Second Sunday of Advent

My kingdom is not of this world. –John 18:36 NIV

I'LL NEVER FORGET THE time during my first year of teaching when I introduced my class to the school's "maintenance engineer." I guess back then I thought a fancy title would make his job sound more important. I didn't want to embarrass him. But Stoney would have none of it.

"Honey, I'm the janitor!" he boomed in a voice that carried all the way down the hall. I was the one who was embarrassed.

Sometimes I still get hung up with titles. After all, nobody likes to feel insignificant. I've had many titles in my lifetime: daughter, sister, wife, mother, grandmother, friend, teacher, writer, editor, musician, Christian. Some have made me feel insignificant—like when I'd spend all day picking up toys, changing diapers, doing laundry, dispensing snacks, making meals, washing dishes, and tending to the million and one mother things, but by day's end, for all my mileage, my house looked as though I hadn't done a thing all day. And the next day

I'd do it all over while my former colleagues left their children with a babysitter, hired a cleaning lady, and went off to work.

In time, though, I got over that. Because I learned that my most important title is Child of God.

Jesus has titles, too, one of which is King. Yet, when He lived on earth, He never looked down on anyone else, He never acted as though He was better than anyone else. Instead God's own Son left the glory of heaven to be born in a barn, laid in a feeding trough, and raised in a poor carpenter's home in a town with a bad reputation. When He grew up, He surrounded Himself with fishermen who lived from hand to mouth and tax collectors who were considered the scum of society. He walked about like a vagrant, having no place to call home. He died between two criminals in front of a mocking crowd and was buried in a borrowed grave. Yet the sign over His cross proclaimed what the wise men knew more than thirty years earlier when they brought Him a gift fit for a king—gold.

He was King then and He is King now, but is He King of your heart?

Jesus, King of kings, reign in my heart today. Amen.

MORE TEA: Read and meditate on John 18:33–19:22.

Like Father, Like Son
Third Sunday of Advent

I and the Father are one. –John 10:30 NIV

WHEN I WAS A young bride, I noticed something peculiar about my new husband: whenever we spent Saturdays visiting his parents on their farm, he was a different person than he was in our apartment in town. On the farm, he walked with a spring in his step, a whistle on his lips, and a twinkle in his eyes. Nothing he could do in town could bring such joy to his heart as riding that old tractor across the hayfields, tinkering around in the wagon shed fixing machinery, or moving dirt from one pile to another. He was just like his father.

I liked this side of him, though, so when it came time to choose a home of our own, we built on land that was once part of the Huey homestead.

As the years passed, I noticed our oldest son, Todd, had this same love for the land that his father has and his grandfather had before him. He spent his childhood exploring the woods, damming up the creek, and helping his dad make hay in the summertime.

Like father, like son.

When Philip asked Jesus, "Show us the Father," he hadn't yet seen the family resemblance.

"Don't you know me, Philip, after I have been among you such a long time?" Jesus answered him. "Anyone who has seen me has seen the Father."

Jesus was—and is—God. And when we finally see the family resemblance, our hearts, too, will turn toward home.

As I light the third Advent candle, dear God, I am reminded that I, too, am part of Your family through Your Son, Jesus. Amen.

MORE TEA: Read and meditate on John 14:8–11.

A Strange Gift
Fourth Sunday of Advent

I am the resurrection and the life; he who believes in Me will live even if he dies. —John 11:25 NASB

MYRRH—WHAT A STRANGE gift for a newborn baby! The bitter-tasting, pungent resin used to make perfume and incense was also used to anoint a body for burial. The word itself means "bitter." Why would the Magi give myrrh as a baby gift? Was it some cruel joke? Or, like the gold and frankincense, did it symbolize something—something too terrible for words?

When we hear the Christmas story, we tend to focus on all the "pretty" things: the angels' songs, the shepherds' adoration, the brilliant star. We'd rather forget the weeping that followed the song when a crazed, power-hungry king killed innocent babies. We forget that, in fear, Mary and Joseph fled to Egypt with the baby Jesus. Yes, we find grief and fear even in the Christmas story.

There are many today who dread the holiday season. Perhaps they've lost a loved one during the past year. Perhaps they or someone they love is facing a life-threatening illness. Perhaps they're scraping the bottom of the barrel financially. Perhaps they'll be spending Christmas alone thousands of miles from home. Like Mary and Martha, who grieved for their dead brother Lazarus, when we're down, we tend to feel only despair.

Yet, in the midst of sorrow, pain, and fear, there is hope and, yes, joy. Because this isn't all there is. Because of Jesus, there's heaven for those who believe in Him. And that's the sweetest—and best—gift of all.

Thank You, Jesus, for the hope You bring into our lives. Amen.

MORE TEA: Read and meditate on John 11:1–44.

What's in the Darkness
First Sunday of Advent

The light shines in the darkness, and the darkness has not overcome it. –John 1:5 RSV

WHEN I WAS A child, I was afraid of the dark. That was because my brother and sister, both older than I, would scare me with ghost stories and hide in the dark, making mysterious noises. I had a vivid imagination even then, and their antics only increased my fear. When I went upstairs at night, I had to flip every light switch along the way, and I couldn't fall asleep unless the hall light at the bottom of the stairs was turned on, its beams reaching into my bedroom, dispelling the darkness and calming my fears.

When I grew up, however, I learned no spooks lurked in the darkness, waiting to harm me, and the darkness held no real threat. But still, inky blackness had the power to resurrect old fears buried deep in the recesses of my heart.

I remember one time my husband, I, and our three children were camping, and all the lights were extinguished. It was so dark I couldn't see my hand two inches from my face. My heart beat faster, and my breath came in short gasps.

"Calm down," I scolded myself. I thought about turning on the reading light and reading through the night until I fell asleep, but the light would disturb my husband. So I squeezed my eyes shut, pulled the covers over my head, and forced myself to breathe deeply and slowly—and think about something other than the blackness that still held terror for me.

While adults may scoff at a child's (or another adult's) fear of the dark, I believe we need to respect it for its power for good and for evil.

The Bible tells us there are three kinds of darkness: Physical darkness is the absence of light and can harbor both good (rest) and bad. Our fears, worries, and heartaches are felt more acutely at night, and loom larger than in the light of the day. Spiritual darkness, not knowing what is right and true, also represents everything evil, gloomy, or hopeless. Eternal darkness is hell, the absence of God.

As Christians, we are to avoid spiritual darkness, respect its power to destroy and send us into eternal darkness, but not fear it. Why?

"I am the light of the world," Jesus tells us in John 8:12. "Whoever follows me will never walk in darkness, but will have the light of life."

Jesus, the Messiah, the only begotten Son of God, the child born in Bethlehem, the God-man who never sinned and became the perfect sacrifice, paying the punishment for our sin by shedding His blood and dying on a cross so that the darkness will no longer have power over us. Jesus, whose name means "God will save," who overcame the eternal darkness of death and rose from the grave, continues to shine in the darkness, and the darkness has not—and cannot ever—overpower Him.

Like that hall light when I was a child, His beams of love and life continue to reach out to me, surrounding me, enfolding me, dispelling the darkness around me, and calming my fears. I know I need never be afraid of the dark anymore.

As I light the first Advent candle, dear God, remind me, in this season of long, dark nights, I never need to fear the dark, as long as I walk in the Light. Amen.

MORE TEA: Read and meditate on John 1:1–18.

Dispelling the Darkness
Second Sunday of Advent

The people that walked in darkness have seen a great light. –Isaiah 9:2 KJV

WE RECENTLY INSTALLED A motion-detecting floodlight on our house facing the driveway. One night it came on and stayed on, instead of automatically shutting off after five minutes.

"The light isn't working right," I told my husband, after flipping the switch several times.

"There must be something out there, setting it off," he told me.

The light is programmed so it remains off until the embedded sensor detects motion in front of it and automatically turns on the floodlight, illuminating the driveway and the surrounding yard. The light is also programmed so it doesn't come on during the day, when there is plenty of natural light to see where you're going.

Even though I couldn't see what was triggering the light, there was something in the darkness beyond the beams of the light the sensor was picking up. So said my husband. But I'm one of those people who have to see it to believe it, so I wasn't sure if I agreed. Since I couldn't see anything, I figured the light was malfunctioning. We couldn't have the thing turning on in the middle of the night every time a deer or some other critter tripped the sensor. We weren't expecting anyone, so I used the manual override feature and turned it off for the night.

But the light does have its advantages. It saves on the electric bill and gives us light to see where we're going when we come home after dark.

Living in this world, we're surrounded by spiritual darkness and will stumble unless we have something to light our way and give us understanding. What can give us spiritual light? There is only one source, God Himself: "The LORD is my light" (Psalm 27:1).

Through His Word He gives us understanding and guides us in the way we are to go: "Your word is a lamp to my feet and a light to my path" (Psalm 119:105).

If that wasn't enough, He sent His Son, Jesus Christ, into this world to make things clearer for us: "I am the light of the world," He said when He was here. "Whoever follows me will never walk in darkness, but will have the light of life" (John 8:12).

Even when He left this world physically and ascended into heaven to sit at the right hand of the Father, He did not leave us in the dark. He gave us the Holy Spirit, the third Person of the Triune God, to guide us into all truth, teach us what we need to know, comfort us, and be with us forever (John 14:16–17, 26; 16:5–15).

Knowing we humans need something we can see and feel, He told us we Christians are to be His lights, shining in this dark world of sin and grief and rebellion: "You are the light of the world. Let your light shine before men, that they may see your good deeds and praise your Father in heaven" (Matthew 5:14–16).

He who is spiritual light created physical light (Genesis 1:3–5), and at the end of time, when physical light is destroyed with the old creation, He Himself will be all the light that is needed: "The city had no need of the sun or of the moon to shine in it, for the glory of the Lord illumined it. The Lamb is its light" (Revelation 21:23). "There will be no more night. They will not need the light of a lamp or the light of the sun, for the Lord God will give them light" (Revelation 22:5).

Yes, much spiritual darkness surrounds us. But God's love is the motion detector that senses our stumbling and groping, reaching for something to show us the way. His light is the only light that will illumine our life's path. When it blazes in the darkness, we can choose to turn it off, walk out of reach of its guiding beams, or stay in the light and follow the only way that will bring us salvation, joy, and eternal life in a place of light forever.

As I light the second Advent candle, Lord God, I am reminded that You are my light and my salvation. Whom shall I fear? No one. What shall I fear? Nothing. Thank You. Amen.

MORE TEA: Read and meditate on Isaiah 9:1–7.

MICHELE HUEY

Christmas Joy
Third Sunday of Advent

Dear Lord, I'm feeling down today,
The bills are stacked up high;
With Christmas just two weeks away,
Our bank account's run dry.
The kids have all presented lists
Of things they want to see;
I hope and pray there's nothing missed
Beneath our Christmas tree.
But I don't have the money for
Expensive clothes and toys;
My credit card can't take much more—
Lord, where's my Christmas joy?
Perhaps it's wrapped up in that hug
My daughter gave this morn;
Or stacked with wood my son did lug
To keep us nice and warm.
Perhaps it's in my oldest's eyes
When he comes home on break
And sees I've baked those pumpkin pies
He wanted me to make.

Perhaps it's in the tired lines
Around my husband's eyes.
Perhaps in love that's grown with time
I've found the greater prize.
A friend who gives a hearty smile,
And cupboards that aren't bare;
And, even if they aren't in style,
I've got *some* clothes to wear.
A family who believes in me
In all things, great and small—
Dear God, I think I finally see
I am not poor at all.

For where your treasure is, there will your heart be also.
–Matthew 6:21 RSV

As I light the third Advent candle—the candle of Joy—I thank You,
Father, for opening my eyes to all that fills my heart with joy. May it
overflow and spill onto everyone around me and infuse all I do and say.
Amen.

Get a Light
Fourth Sunday of Advent

I have come into this world as a light, so that no one who believes in me should stay in darkness. —John 12:46 NIV

AH, CHRISTMAS! ONE SONGWRITER called it the most wonderful time of the year. It's the time for sleigh bells and jingle bells, mistletoe and holly, cookies and parties, angels and mangers. Yet for all the Christmas cheer, it can also herald the most down time of the year.

For those who suffer from SAD, or Seasonal Affective Disorder, the long dark nights trigger the release of melatonin, a sleep-related hormone that can plunge them into a winter-long bout with depression. Symptoms, which can be mild to debilitating, include episodes of depression, excessive eating and sleeping, weight gain, and a craving for sugary and starchy foods. The months of January and February, for those who live in the Northern Hemisphere, are the worst. The symptoms subside in the spring and summer months.

From the fall equinox in September, when the daylight hours equal the nighttime hours, until the winter solstice on December 21 or 22, the days get shorter and the nights get longer.

That's because, as the earth rotates on its axis and revolves around the sun, it also tilts toward or away from the sun. During the fall and winter months, the Northern Hemisphere gradually tilts away from the sun, and the climate turns colder. Plants lose their leaves and go dormant, appearing lifeless until the earth tilts toward the sun again in the spring and summer months. Then what appeared dead during the winter bursts with new life, warmth and color return, and people find renewed energy and enthusiasm.

I used to joke about my winter weight and summer weight, and my tendency to want to hibernate during the long winter months. But I've learned to recognize the symptoms and deal with them to avoid having to work off all that extra weight when my energy returns in the spring.

The therapy for SAD is simple: more exposure to light, especially natural light. An hour's walk in the winter sunlight, one study found, is as effective as two and a half hours under bright artificial light.

In our spiritual lives, we, too, have seasons of darkness and light, times when we lean and reach toward the Son and times when we tilt away from Him. During the winter of the soul, our spirits are lifeless and colorless. The further we get from the Son, the colder our hearts grow. We feed on things not healthy to our spiritual well-being. The more we consume, the more we want. It's a downward cycle halted only when we realize what's happening, decide we don't want to live in the dark and cold anymore, and turn toward the Son.

Just as the remedy for Seasonal Affective Disorder is exposure to more light, so the remedy for our Spiritual Affective Disorder, also called sin, is exposure to the Light of the World, the Son of God, Jesus Christ, the Second Person of the Triune God, who left the light of the Father and heaven to come to earth and take the punishment for our sin so that we may live in the light forever.

"I am the light of the world," the Son said. "Whoever follows me will never walk in darkness, but will have the light of life" (John 8:12).

"In Him was life," wrote John the Apostle, "and that life was the light of men."

Just like in the physical world, where's there's light, there's life. Do you have that Light? Do you have eternal life?

If not, turn toward Him today and celebrate, not only the earthly birth of the Son, but also new life in Him (John 3). Celebrate your spiritual birthday this Christmas.

As I light the fourth Advent candle, dear Lord, I am thankful that You left the glories of heaven to spread Your light in this dark world. Thank You for the light that gives life to my soul. Amen.

MORE TEA: Read and meditate on 1 John 1.

The Lesson of the Begats

All Scripture is inspired by God and is useful to teach us what is true and to make us realize what is wrong with our lives. It straightens us out and teaches us to do what is right. It is God's way of preparing us in every way, fully equipped for every good thing God wants us to do. –2 Timothy 3:16–17 NLT

ARE YOU GUILTY OF skipping the "begats"?

The "begats" to which I refer are found in the first chapter of Matthew—you know, the long list of Jesus' ancestors. I don't know about you, but when I read, I like action. History never stuck with me, especially long lists of names I can't even pronounce, let alone see why they're important.

I, too, am guilty of passing over the begats. But one time I forced myself to read through them—only because I was following a read-through-the-Bible-in-one-year program and putting a check mark in the "Matthew 1" box without actually reading it was cheating, lying, and being deceitful. I knew it would prey on my conscience, so I plowed through.

And discovered something interesting: Jesus' ancestors were not a saintly bunch. Up until then, I'd assumed that Jesus, who was sinless and pure, would have had a bloodline that reflected his holiness. Yet "holy" hardly describes some of the characters mentioned. I'd also assumed that his bloodline would be pure as well—all His ancestors would have been Jewish. I was wrong on that account, too.

Jesus' ancestry includes people who lied, cheated, deceived, stole, and committed adultery and murder. Abraham lied on at least two occasions to save his own skin. Jacob, whose name means "deceitful," lived up to his name. Judah thought nothing of sleeping with a woman he thought was a prostitute. Bathsheba, Solomon's mother, committed adultery with King David, who had her husband murdered when he discovered she was pregnant with his child.

Rahab was a prostitute from Jericho and not an Israelite. Neither was Ruth, King David's great-grandmother. She hailed from Moab—Israel's one-time enemy, a nation birthed in incest, whose bloodline traced back to Lot, who slept with his own daughters. Then there was the shrewd and perseverant Tamar, whose twins were begotten in deceit.

Talk about skeletons in your closet! Jesus sure had plenty in His ancestry.

Another interesting note in the genealogy Matthew recorded is that he included women. It was unusual for women to be listed in Jewish genealogies. Matthew, however, lists five: Tamar, Rahab, Ruth, Bathsheba, and Mary. Only two were Jewish. Three bore moral blots.

Over the next few readings, we're going to look at the stories of these five women, the role they played in Jewish history, and what it means for us today.

Everything in God's Word has a purpose, even the accounts of unsavory characters whom God chose to fill a slot in the ancestry of His own Son.

What's the message you see in this? That God doesn't choose only men to fulfill His purposes? That allowing far-from-perfect men—and women—a part in His plan to save sinners is still more evidence of His amazing grace? Nobody's perfect, but surely there were people with better moral records than these. That God makes good on His promises, even one made four thousand years before it was fulfilled?

For me, seeing the names of some pretty unsavory characters whose treachery and deceit are chronicled in the archives of man gave me a sense of relief and freedom.

Relief that I don't have to be perfect—God can use me warts and all. And freedom from guilt that my past indiscretions will cause me to miss out on God's purpose for me.

For God, you see, "has saved us and called us to a holy life—*not because of anything we have done*, but because of his own purpose and grace" (2 Timothy 1:9 NIV, emphasis mine).

Skeletons in your closet? Don't fret about them. It isn't what's in your closet that God's concerned about—it's what's in your heart.

Thank you, God, for the lesson of the begats. Amen.

MORE TEA: Read and meditate on Matthew 1.

Tamar's Trump Card

*Judah the father of Perez and Zerah, whose mother was Tamar. –
Matthew 1:3 NIV*

*Many are the plans in a man's heart, but it is the LORD's purpose
that prevails. –Proverbs 19:21 NIV*

ONE OF THE SKELETONS in Jesus' genealogical closet was a
woman by the name of Tamar, the Canaanite wife of Judah's
oldest son, Er.

At that time, the sons of Israel weren't a nation yet. They
were a bickering, jealous, scheming lot who sold their own
brother into slavery. Judah's was the line that would eventually
produce the Messiah. You'd think it would be a line that was
pure and noble, filled with brave men and women who did what
was right.

Think again.

Now, Judah's son Er was so wicked God put him to death.
Since Er had no sons, his widow, Tamar, was given to his
brother Onan, Judah's second son. This was the custom back in
those days to keep the family line going. Problem was, if Onan
fathered a son, the boy wouldn't legally be his—it would be his
dead brother's.

That didn't go over too well with Onan. So he made sure he wouldn't sire a child through Tamar. That didn't go over too well with God, who zapped him, too.

"Live as a widow in your father's house until my son Shelah grows up," Judah told Tamar. But he had no intention of giving his remaining son to a woman who went through two of his offspring already.

Tamar did what she was told. She went to her father's house and waited. And waited. And waited. Eventually she realized she'd be a widow in her father's house until the day she died if she waited for Judah to make good on his word. So she took matters into her own hands.

Disguising herself as a prostitute, she sat down by the roadside when she knew he'd be passing by. Her plan worked. Judah "hired" her.

"What will you give me?" she asked.

"A young goat from my flock," he said.

"Will you give me something as a pledge until you send it?"

"What do you want?" he asked.

"Your seal and your cord and the staff in your hand."

Without a thought he handed them over.

Shrewd of Tamar. Stupid of Judah. These items were the driver's licenses and Social Security numbers of that day, used for identification.

When Judah sent a servant with the promised goat, he couldn't find her.

"There hasn't been any shrine prostitute here," the men of the area told him.

"Ah, let her keep what she has," Judah said when the servant reported back to him.

Three months later Judah learned Tamar was pregnant. Furious, indignant, he called for her to be burned to death. She played her trump card.

"See if you recognize whose seal and cord and staff these are," she said. "I am pregnant by the man who owns them."

Ever want to get away? I'm sure Judah did at that moment.

"She is more righteous than I, since I wouldn't give her to my son Shelah," he said.

One of the twin boys she bore, Perez, would be an ancestor of Jesus, the Messiah.

This isn't a story of "all's well that ends well." Neither is it evidence that "the end justifies the means." And don't claim Romans 8:28—"all things work together for good." "Good" isn't "best."

But to fulfill His promise, God used the only thing He had—flawed human beings who thought nothing of shirking their duty, going back on their word, and obtaining what they wanted through deception and manipulation.

Human nature hasn't changed. But what has changed is that now we can do something about it. For God "has saved us and called us to a holy life—*not because of anything we have done*, but because of his own purpose and grace" (2 Timothy 1:9 NIV, emphasis mine).

And that's a trump card in anybody's hand.

"Amazing grace, how sweet the sound that saved a wretch like me! I once was lost, but now am found, was blind but now I see."* Thank You, thank You, thank You, Lord! Amen.

*From "Amazing Grace," by John Newton, Public Domain.

MORE TEA: Read and meditate on Genesis 38:6–30.

Of Prostitutes and Promises

Salmon the father of Boaz, whose mother was Rahab . . . –Matthew 1:5 NIV

Was not even Rahab the prostitute considered righteous for what she did when she gave lodging to the spies and sent them off in a different direction? –James 2:25 NIV

By faith the prostitute Rahab, because she welcomed the spies, was not killed with those who were disobedient. –Hebrews 11:31 NIV

THE YEAR: CIRCA 1400 BC. The place: Jericho, the most fortified city in the land of Canaan.

Having served their sentence of forty years in the wilderness, the Israelites were knocking at Jericho's gates. Even though God's chosen people were still on the other side of the Jordan River, the inhabitants of Jericho, ten thousand strong, were terrified. They'd heard all about how the Red Sea miraculously parted so the children of Israel could walk through on dry ground and how the pursuing Egyptians drowned. They'd heard about how the Israelites, a fugitive nation with little or no military training, had annihilated the Amorite kingdoms of kings Sihon and Og.

And now, here they were, just across the river, poised to strike. Yep, the citizens of Jericho were shaking in their sandals.

But the Israelites didn't know this. Not until Joshua, their leader, sent two spies to the city. It should come as no surprise that these men ended up in the house of the only person in Jericho who would protect them—a prostitute by the name of Rahab.

When the king sent his heavies to Rahab's house to arrest the spies, she said they'd already left.

"If you hurry," she told them, "you can catch up with them."

Then she went up to the roof, where the spies were hiding under stalks of flax laid out for drying.

"I know that the LORD has given this land to you and that a great fear of you has fallen on us, so that all who live in this country are melting in fear because of you," she said. "Everyone's courage failed because of you, for the LORD your God is God of heaven above and on the earth below."

Her words jogged their memory: "I will put the terror and fear of you on all the nations under heaven," God had promised not too long before. "They will hear reports of you and will tremble and be in anguish because of you" (Deuteronomy 2:25 NIV).

Rahab then asked for protection for her and her family when they conquered the city. The spies promised, tying a scarlet cord in the window that would identify her house to the invading Israelites.

You know what happened. The walls of Jericho fell down flat, the Israelites conquered and burned the city, and Rahab and her family were saved.

But did you know that Rahab, the former harlot, married Salmon, who is believed to be the son of Caleb, one of the two spies who came back with a good report forty years earlier? The union of their son Boaz and Ruth produced Obed, the grandfather of King David, an ancestor of Jesus the Messiah.

This is a story of faith and faithfulness: the remarkable faith of Rahab, which distinguished her for the future "Hall of Faith" (Hebrews 11), and the faithfulness of God, who always keeps His promises.

Take note: Jericho fell a few weeks after the flax was harvested—in March, the time of the Passover. The crimson blood of the Passover lamb represented a promise, a covenant, between God and the Israelites. The scarlet cord in Rahab's window identified the one to whom a promise was made.

Fast-forward 1,400 years, to the night one of Rahab's descendants, a man named Jesus, held up a cup of wine, and proclaimed, "This is My blood of the new covenant . . ."

This blood, the blood of God's only Son, fulfilled the promise He made at the dawn of civilization, when the sin of our first parents created a chasm between them, and hence all mankind, and a loving Creator.

If Rahab, a common prostitute who lived in a nation whose wickedness aroused God's wrath and marked them for total destruction, could believe the promises of a God she'd only heard of at the risk of her life, how can we, who have God's Word and His Spirit, not also believe?

"Come, thou long-expected Jesus, born to set thy people free. From our fears and sins release us; let us find our rest in thee. Israel's strength and consolation, hope of all the earth thou art. Dear desire of every nation, joy of every longing heart."*

*From "Come, Thou Long-Expected Jesus," by Charles Wesley, Public Domain.

MORE TEA: Read and meditate on Joshua 2.

Famines, Funerals, and Families

. . . Salmon the father of Boaz, whose mother was Rahab, Boaz the father of Obed, whose mother was Ruth, Obed the father of Jesse, and Jesse the father of King David. –Matthew 1:5–6 NIV

And we know that in all things God works for the good of those who love him, who have been called according to his purpose. –Romans 8:28 NIV

ELEVEN HUNDRED YEARS BEFORE Jesus' birth, there lived in Bethlehem of Judea an Israelite named Elimelech. A famine struck the land, and Elimelech took his wife, Naomi, and two sons, Mahlon and Kilion, to Moab, a land east of the Dead Sea where grain was abundant.

Now, Moab wasn't on Israel's friends list. In fact, they were bitter enemies. (For the whole sordid story, read Genesis 19:30–36 and Numbers 22–25.) But Moab was where the food was.

The sons took Moabite wives, Orpah and Ruth. In time Elimelech died. Then Mahlon and Kilion also died. All this in the span of a decade.

There were no career paths or jobs outside the home for women at that time. No Social Security, no IRAs. Unless she was well off, a widow faced a future of poverty and had to depend on the charity of relatives. Naomi, whose name means "pleasant," determined it was time to return home, where the famine was finally over, and where her late husband had relatives. Orpah and Ruth would accompany her.

Along the way, however, Naomi realized her daughters-in-law's plight: As Moabite widows living in Israel, they had little, if any, chance of ever remarrying. The "kinsman-redeemer" practice of levirate marriage, in which the widow marries her dead husband's brother to produce a son in his name so the family line doesn't die out, wouldn't help them. Naomi was too old to have any more sons.

"Go back home," she urged them. There they could remarry, have children, and not face a life of poverty.

Orpah, in tears, kissed Naomi goodbye and returned to her pagan homeland. But Ruth made a surprising choice.

"Don't urge me to leave you," she said. "Where you go I will go, and where you stay I will stay. Your people will be my people and your God my God. Where you die I will die, and there I will be buried. May the LORD deal with me, be it ever so severely, if anything but death separates you and me" (Ruth 1:16–17 NIV).

Naomi's faithfulness to God while living in a heathen nation had made an impact on her daughters-in-law, whether she realized it or not. But now she wondered if this was how God rewarded faithfulness.

"Could this be Naomi?" the womenfolk exclaimed when she returned to Bethlehem.

"Don't call me Naomi," the grieving woman said. "Call me 'Mara' (*Mara* means *bitter*), for the Almighty has made my life very bitter. I went away full, but the LORD brought me back empty."

You know the rest of the story. How Ruth "just happened" to glean in the fields belonging to a wealthy relative of her late father-in-law. How Boaz redeemed Elimelech's inheritance, taking Ruth as his wife. And how Naomi's life became full again when she bounced her new grandson, Obed, on her knee.

She didn't know that this grandson would be an ancestor of the Promised Messiah. All she knew was that God had turned her mourning into dancing, her sorrow into joy.

According to tradition, the Field of Boaz, where Ruth gleaned after the harvesters, where Boaz first set eyes on Ruth, is the field where, eleven hundred years later, an angel appeared to shepherds and made a startling birth announcement. And the house where Boaz took Ruth to be his wife, a millennium later, was the site of a stable where a virgin from Nazareth gave birth to the Son of God.

Have you, like Naomi, cried out in the depths of grief, disappointment, and pain? "God, how could You let this happen? Haven't I been faithful?"

Just wait. Like Naomi, God works in *all* things for your good (Romans 8:28). He will turn your bitter, crushing losses into joy unspeakable. He promised. And God always keeps His promises.

All you have to do is believe.

When disappointments and sorrows and trials come and linger, remind me, dear Lord, of Your promise—that You will work all things for good. Amen.

MORE TEA: Read and meditate on the Book of Ruth.

Bathing Beauty or Bimbo?

David was the father of Solomon, whose mother had been Uriah's wife. –Matthew 1:6 NIV

"For my thoughts are not your thoughts, neither are your ways my ways," declares the LORD. "For as the heavens are higher than the earth, so are my ways higher than your ways and my thoughts than your thoughts."–Isaiah 55:8–9 NIV

ALTHOUGH SHE'S ONE OF five women having the honor of being in mentioned in Jesus' genealogy, unlike the other four, Bathsheba's name is not given. Matthew simply refers her to as "Uriah's wife."

In my humble opinion, she's worse than Tamar and Rahab. She can't even hold a candle to Ruth, whose story is like a polished diamond in the coal mines of the Old Testament. They had what Bathsheba lacked—brains, guts, and heart.

When we first encounter Bathsheba, she's taking a bath—in an uncovered courtyard of a house in the middle of Jerusalem, where anyone standing on a nearby rooftop (they were flat in those days) could see her. Perhaps that was her intention. You see, the courtyard where she was bathing was in plain sight of the rooftop of King David's residence. Scripture tells us Bathsheba was very beautiful

Now King David already had seven wives, including Saul's daughter Michal, the wife of his youth, and Abigail, the spunky, quick-witted widow of Nabal. (Read this great story in 1 Samuel 25.) Nevertheless, he summons Bathsheba, knowing both her husband and her father are members of the elite group of warriors known as "David's mighty men."

She could have said no. She knew the commandments as well as King David did. But she didn't.

You know the story. Bathsheba gets pregnant and David arranges for a combat fatality. As soon the seven days of mourning for her husband Uriah are up, Bathsheba marries King David. The baby conceived in adultery dies soon after birth.

Fast-forward to the end of David's life. As he lay on his deathbed, his son Adonijah plans to usurp the throne. David's chief prophet approaches Bathsheba with a plan.

"Go in to King David and say to him, 'Didn't you promise me my son Solomon would be king after you? Then why has Adonijah become king?'"

She does as told. Solomon is crowned that very day (1 Kings 1:11–39). Okay, so she secured the throne for the king God had planned. But it wasn't her idea.

The last time we see Bathsheba, she's the queen mother. The relentless Adonijah uses her in a plot to wrest the throne from Solomon.

"Ask him to do one thing for me," Adonijah tells her. "Give me Abishag the Shunammite as my wife."

"Very well," she says.

Was she that clueless as to what this meant? She should have known. Abishag was a part of David's harem, and possession of the previous king's harem signified the right of succession to the throne. By marrying Abishag, Adonijah would strengthen his claim to the throne. Good thing Solomon saw through the scheme.

Bathsheba possessed great physical beauty, but little else. If it had been up to me, I would have chosen Abigail, who had more character, intelligence, and spunk, for the honor of being an ancestor of the Messiah.

But God didn't ask for my opinion.

Bathsheba bore David four sons, which included Solomon and Nathan. The wise and wealthy Solomon became one of Jesus' ancestors through Joseph, his earthly father. Nathan's line produced Mary, Jesus' mother (Luke 3:31).

Bathsheba—bathing beauty or bimbo? Does it even matter?

What matters is that God chose her, not because of anything she did, but because of His own purpose and grace (2 Timothy 1:9 NIV) to fulfill a promise He made to David: "Your house and your kingdom will endure forever before me; your throne will be established forever" (2 Samuel 7:16 NIV).

This promise was fulfilled with Jesus' birth, death, and resurrection.

Bathsheba's story is one of mercy and grace. Mercy, because she didn't get the punishment she deserved for her adultery and her part in David's conspiracy to murder her husband. Grace, because she received something she didn't deserve—a place in the bloodline of Jesus Christ.

Mercy and grace—isn't that what God's all about?

"Thy steadfast love, O LORD, extends to the heavens, thy faithfulness to the clouds" (Psalm 36:5). Remind me of this, dear God, when I question Your love for and Your faithfulness to me. Amen.

MORE TEA: Read and meditate on 2 Samuel 11:1–12:24.

Mary

. . . and Jacob the father of Joseph, the husband of Mary, of whom was born Jesus, who is called the Christ. –Matthew 1:16 NIV

"And a sword will pierce your own soul too." –Luke 2:35 NIV

THE LAST WOMAN TO be named in "the begats" of the first chapter of Matthew, Mary was a far cry from the other four. Unlike Tamar, Rahab, and Ruth, Mary, from the tribe of Judah and of the lineage of David, was thoroughbred Jewish. And unlike Tamar, Rahab, and Bathsheba, Mary was pure in every way—body, mind, heart, and soul.

Other than her role in the Christmas story, what do we know of her?

We know that she was probably a young teenager when the angel Gabriel appeared to her to tell her that she was to be the mother of the Messiah. We know that she grew up in Nazareth, a disreputable town of about seven thousand in the hills of Galilee. We know that she was betrothed to a carpenter named Joseph, also from Nazareth, who was probably about thirty years of age.

We know that Joseph was a good man, just and sensitive, and who most likely died before Jesus entered public ministry.

We know that she, still a virgin, gave birth to the Son of God in a stable in Bethlehem with her husband as the midwife. We know they were too poor to afford the lamb required for the sacrifice when she went to the temple forty days after Jesus' birth for the purification ceremony.

We know that she spent the first couple of years of her married life as a fugitive, hiding in Egypt from a crazy king who was set on killing her Son.

After their return to Nazareth following Herod's death, we see Mary briefly only five more times in Scripture: in the temple in Jerusalem when she admonished twelve-year-old Jesus for staying behind after the Passover and not telling them (Luke 2:41–52); at the wedding in Cana, where, at her request, Jesus performed his first recorded miracle (John 2:1–5); in Capernaum when she and her other sons tried to see Jesus but received not a welcome but a rebuff (Matthew 12:46–50; Mark 3:21, 31–34; Luke 8:18); at the foot of the cross, watching her Son die a horrific death (John 10:25–27); and in the upper room with the apostles after Jesus' ascension into heaven (Acts 1:14).

No special privileges came with being the mother of God's Son. Her acceptance of Gabriel's message meant possible disgrace, divorce, and even death, as those guilty of having sex outside of marriage were stoned. After her burst of worship in the famous "Magnificat," she steps humbly and submissively into the background.

She feared for her Son's life when He was but a baby. She raised Him, nurtured Him, trained Him in the way He should go, admonished Him, tried to intervene when His schedule was so heavy He had no time to eat, watched Him die like a common criminal in the most public, humiliating way.

As Simeon predicted when Jesus was a mere infant, a sword, indeed, pierced her mother's soul.

No special privileges except to bear and raise the Son of God—then, like all mothers eventually do, let Him go.

I often think I deserve special privileges because I've been obedient. I pray about what I think are unmet needs: the kitchen floor (a painted subfloor), the roof that needs to be replaced, the two aging vehicles in our driveway.

But God reminds me I have much more than Mary, whose floor was probably dirt and who doubtless didn't even have a donkey for travel. I have a roof over my head, a warm, dry bed to sleep in, enough vegetables and meat (venison) to feed me and my husband for a year. My husband has a steady job. We are both relatively healthy.

Yes, God promises blessings for obedience. But sometimes I'm blind to the real blessings because I'm too focused on the wrong things.

As the Christmas season eases into the New Year, I pray God will give me the eyes to see His blessings, the ears to hear His commands, the mouth to praise Him, the mind and soul to know Him, the heart to love Him, and the desire to serve Him.

Open my eyes, O Lord, to Your abiding presence in my life, Your abundant provision, Your awesome plan, and Your able protection. Thank You for reminding me that I'm not poor at all. Amen.

MORE TEA: Read and meditate on Luke 1:26–56.

Symbols of Christmas

Every good and perfect gift is from above,
coming down from the Father of lights.

–James 1:17 ESV

Why Mistletoe?

We love, because He first loved us. –1 John 4:19 AMP

I HAD A DOOZY of a time finding mistletoe this year. Maybe it was because I was looking for it Sunday morning before church so I could use it in my sermon, "The Symbols of Christmas."

That, and I still needed to get a sprig to hang on the ceiling beam between the kitchen and the dining room, which has become a Christmas tradition in our home. Truth be told, rarely does anyone smooch under it. But I still like to hang it up.

How did mistletoe, a symbol of love (which we celebrate on Valentine's Day), become associated with Christmas?

Legends about this evergreen plant go back to the ancient Druids of Britain, who believed mistletoe had special healing powers and used it in their winter solstice ceremonies. Actually, "mistletoe," in the Celtic language, means "all heal."

When Christianity took root, pagan practices and beliefs were condemned, and mistletoe was all but forgotten until the 1800s, when Victorian England revived the tradition of kissing under the mistletoe as a sign of love, romance, and good luck.

When I researched mistletoe for information for my sermon, I discovered it's actually an aerial parasite, having no roots of its own. To survive, mistletoe attaches itself to a tree, from which it gets its nourishment.

Like love.

Love, whether romantic love or brotherly love, doesn't exist on its own. All love originates from, and gets its nourishment from, *agape* love—divine love. Agape is the highest form of love, transcending all other types of love. It is the love of God for man—unconditional, unlimited, sacrificial, selfless, giving of itself regardless of circumstances. God's love is the tree that sustains us—physically, spiritually, emotionally, mentally.

Interestingly, agape, pronounced a-GÁP-ē, can also be pronounced ə'gāp, which refers to the mouth when it is "wide open with wonder and surprise."

Such is the love God has for us—it should leave us with mouths wide open in wonder and surprise that the God who created the universe—the King of kings and Lord of lords—loved each of us so much He left His throne in heaven to take on human flesh, live a sinless life and give Himself up as the perfect sacrifice to pay the price for our sins so we could live in heaven with Him forever (see John 3:16).

Such is the love of God.

And like the mistletoe is an evergreen, so God's love is eternal—it always was and always will be (Psalm 136). It's unlimited (Psalm 36:5, 108:4). And it is mine.

God's is the love from which all other love springs and is sustained. We love, you see, because He first loved us (1 John 4:19). And like the mistletoe cannot survive without being attached to the tree, so our love cannot sustain itself. God's love is the tree that feeds us, gives us life, and enables us to love.

And just like the meaning of mistletoe is "all heal," God's love is the healing salve we need for all our wounds—physical, mental, emotional, spiritual.

Wow. All that about a sprig of evergreen we hang up in our homes at Christmastime and, for the most part, forget about.

A sprig of evergreen that reminds us of the love God has for each one of us—nourishing, life-giving, and eternal.

May each sprig of mistletoe I see this Christmas season, O God, remind me of the love that sent Your Son from heaven to earth so that we may have heaven forever. Amen.

MORE TEA: Read and meditate on 1 John 4:7–21.

More than Just a Decoration

Those who hope in the LORD will renew their strength. They will soar on wings like eagles; they will run and not grow weary, they will walk and not be faint. –Isaiah 40:31 NIV

EVEN THOUGH MY HUSBAND brought down the Christmas decorations from the attic two weeks earlier than usual, putting them up is taking longer this year.

It might be because we are slowing down. It might be because our family will no longer gather at our house on Christmas Eve to enjoy a meal together and exchange presents. That tradition, sad to say, has disappeared into the land of Christmas Past.

Life changes. It's dynamic, not static. Which really is a good thing because the only things that don't change are dead. So I accept the life changes. Even if I don't like them. Even though I miss the wonderful chaos that was Christmas Eve at our house.

So, why decorate when there's just the two of us?

Because there are two of us. And we will celebrate the birth of our Savior because He came to give us something we all need: hope.

Which brings me to the pine cone.

This year, it's more than a decoration to me.

Why?

Because it symbolizes hope.

I learned something about the pine cone this past summer on our road trip to the Pacific Northwest.

We were blessed with an amazing guide when we took the bus tour of the Road to the Sun in Glacier National Park. Most tour guides spout off what they have in their minds because they've memorized the script.

Not Jeremiah. He spoke from what was in his heart. His love for the area and for sharing tidbits of information was obvious. There wasn't a question he couldn't answer.

After driving through an area that had been devastated by forest fires, he held up a pine cone.

"The intense heat from a forest fire causes the pine cone to open up. Inside are the seeds of new trees," he explained. "The forest you see around you grew from those seeds that were once inside the pine cones."

If you've ever seen the devastation left by a fire, you'd think all was lost.

But God planned for life to continue. Our Creator placed the seeds of new life within the pine cone and made it so that an all-consuming fire wouldn't destroy that new life, but initiate it.

Wow.

The forest would never be the same as it was before the fire, but new life emerged from the ashes of the old.

Only God.

There are times in our lives when we are left in the ruins of our hopes and dreams. We stumble through the valley of desolation, darkness without, discouragement and disillusionment within. Our hope is gone.

So we think.

But take a lesson from the pine cone: hope is never gone. Not when you've made the sovereign God your God (see Romans 8:28).

A new life will grow from the ashes of your hopes and dreams. A new dream. New hope that will carry you through when your faith is weak.

The pine cone—it's more than a decoration. It's a reminder of hope.

How I need hope, O Lord! Rekindle the fire of hope in my heart, mind, and spirit. Amen.

MORE TEA: Read and meditate on Isaiah 40:21–31.

Following the Star

Once again the star appeared to them, guiding them to Bethlehem. It went ahead of them and stopped over the place where the child was. – Matthew 2:9 NLT

WHEN I WAS A child, Christmas Eve was a magical time. Perhaps it was the air of excitement and anticipation. Perhaps it was the lights on the Christmas tree, casting a soft glow on the darkened living room throughout the long evenings. Perhaps it was the carols we sang. Perhaps it was the Christmas story itself, with all its mystery and awe.

Maybe that's what made Christmas Eve so magical: I accepted without reservation the Christmas story in its entirety—from a virgin giving birth to the Son of God in a stable, to angels announcing the birth to lowly shepherds, to a bright star leading the Magi to Jesus. I understood that whatever science or nature could not explain, God could. After all, He is the Creator and set the laws of nature in motion. No doubt poisoned Christmas for me.

These days, however, there are those who would remove the reason for the season, who scoff at the miracles and spoil the magic, who reject that which cannot be explained except by the touch of God.

The Magi, learned men from the East, could have scoffed, too. But they didn't reject what their own eyes saw—a colossal star with a radiance that shone even during the day. These astronomer–mathematicians recognized the importance of this brilliant star that appeared at the time of Jesus' birth.

But how did these heathen Gentiles, these nonbelievers, know that a Jewish king was born?

Familiar with the prophecies of Daniel, who was an exile in their land hundreds of years earlier, these wise men who studied the heavens knew the Jews were waiting for a Messiah promised by God Himself, someone who would save them and rule them forever.

They knew the Hebrews considered the constellation Pisces as representing their own nation. The planet Saturn, viewed as a wandering star, represented Jerusalem, their capital city. Jupiter, another "wandering star," denoted royalty.

When Jupiter and Saturn converged in Pisces three times in two months, the wise men knew something big was about to happen. This astronomical event normally occurred only once every 804 years. Then a few months later, Mars joined Jupiter and Saturn in the constellation.

As they puzzled over the meaning of this, they noted the first time this happened was on the Jewish Day of Atonement. Putting all this together, they reasoned that a Hebrew king was about to be born in Judea.

Then, another amazing event occurred: a brilliant new star appeared in the constellation Aquila (the eagle), brighter than anything they'd ever seen, so intense it could be seen in the daytime. To the wise men, this brilliant new star, actually an exploding star called a nova, was the announcement they were waiting for: the King of the Jews had been born.

A king whose birth even the heavens proclaimed was a king they had to see. So they prepared for the long trip to Bethlehem, where they found the infant king. They didn't doubt when they found the child not in a palace but in a humble house. They didn't doubt when they saw how poor His parents were.

They believed what most Jews in that day weren't even aware of—that this child was both a King and a God. When they presented their costly gifts—gifts denoting royalty—they worshiped Him.

For these astronomical events to come together at the very time Jesus was born, for Gentile magi to recognize the significance of it all, for this star to lead them to the exact location of the child they were seeking can only be explained by the touch of the Divine—God reaching out and making the impossible happen.

The wise men, nonbelievers, believed the miracle in the sky and followed that star until it led them to the Savior.

What about you? Are you following that star?

Jesus, when the wise men saw the star that led to You, they rejoiced with "exceedingly great joy." Fill me with this joy every day as I follow the star that leads to You. Amen.

MORE TEA: Read and meditate on Matthew 2:1-12.

Angels From the Realms of Glory

Are not all angels ministering spirits sent to serve those who will inherit salvation? –Hebrews 1:14 NIV

I DON'T COLLECT ANGELS. They come to me.

One of the first angels I received as a gift from my husband's employer at a company Christmas party over twenty-five years ago. The "Satterlee angel," as I came to call her, is a clear, lighted angel about eight inches high, holding a golden banner reading "Merry Christmas." A golden halo once perched above her head. I placed her where she could light up a dark section of the house.

Winter days are often sunless and dreary. Nights are long and darker than any other time of the year. But my Satterlee angel reminds me that, even in the longest, darkest, and coldest times of our lives, God sends us hope in the rays of His Son, which wrap themselves around us, warming the cold places in our hearts and spirits, lighting the darkest paths that stretch before us.

My Satterlee angel represents HOPE.

Then there's my "Donora angel." This angel is one of a pair that my late sister, Judi, had (Judi was the one who gave her the name "Donora angel"). We grew up in that steel mill town in the heart of the Mon Valley. My niece sent her to me the Christmas following my sister's sudden death in August 2003.

My Donora angel is a little over twelve inches high, dressed warmly in a burgundy winter gown with a Christmas-colored plaid apron, red cord belt, and a dark blue shawl. Her beige linen wings fan out behind her tranquil face. Over one arm is draped a Christmas wreath. In her hand she holds an empty birdcage, with a bird perched on top.

My Donora angel reminds me of a past rich with family and traditions and people who helped to mold me into what I am today. People who knew me raw and still believed in me.

My Donora angel represents LOVE.

Another of my eleven angels perched on a shelf on the stairway landing is my "Birthday angel." She was a gift from my little flock after my first tenure of filling the pulpit of that little church in Punxsutawney. A delicate ceramic angel, she wears a necklace with my birthstone, topaz, on a chain around her neck. "November"—my birth month—borders the hem of her gown in raised letters across the bottom. And her halo—oh, my, one little bump and it's askew.

She reminds me of the happiness I get from serving my little flock and serving God in whatever way I can.

My Birthday angel represents JOY.

The most recent angel came to me as a birthday gift from my closest friend, Sharon. Butterflies and flower petals cover her dress. Her wings are framed in gold. The letters across the front of her gown read, "It is such a blessing to have a friend like you."

She is my "Friendship angel," reminding me that friends are gifts from God. They remind us that we are never alone. Our Abba Father sends them to minster to us in times of need, to lend an ear and a helping hand, to give us hugs. Friends stand in the gap for us. A true friend brings a sense of stability and security to our hearts and lives.

My Friendship angel represents PEACE.

Look around. I'll bet you have a few angels watching over you, too.

Thank you, Father, for sending Your angels to minister and watch over me and those I love. Amen.

MORE TEA: Read and meditate on Matthew 1:18–2:23; Luke 1:5–2:20.

Christmas

For unto us a Child is born,
Unto us a Son is given . . .
And His name will be called
Wonderful, Counselor, Mighty God,
Everlasting Father, Prince of Peace.

–Isaiah 9:6 NKJV

The Last Candle

She will give birth to a son, and you are to give him the name Jesus, because he will save his people from their sins. . . . and they will call him Immanuel—which means, "God with us." –Matthew 1:21, 23 NIV

For unto us a child is born, to us a son is given . . . And he will be called Wonderful Counselor, Mighty God, Everlasting Father, Prince of Peace. –Isaiah 9:6 NIV

IT WASN'T A GOOD Christmas for Henry. His oldest son had been badly wounded in the war. And it was another Christmas without his beloved wife Fanny, who died three and a half years earlier as a result of burns suffered in a fire that Henry himself tried to extinguish. The scars from the burns he received while trying to save her made shaving too painful, so he grew a beard—a constant reminder of his tragic loss.

Henry was all too familiar with grief. His first wife died at the age of twenty-two, days after a miscarriage while they were traveling abroad. He'd buried a year-old daughter and a twenty-year-old sister. His grief that Christmas after his son was wounded drove him to pen the following words: "And in despair I bowed my head, 'There is no peace on earth,' I said, 'For hate is strong and mocks the song of peace on earth, good will to men.'"

The year was 1864. The war was the Civil War. The poet was Henry Wadsworth Longfellow.

Times haven't changed much, have they? The country is still at war. Our young men and women are still being wounded. And people still carry burdens of unbearable grief, especially at Christmastime. A season that should be joyful is, for many folks, a reminder of what they have lost.

I didn't set out to write something that would depress you, especially at Christmas time. But I know many of you are coping with grief. Perhaps this is the first year without your husband or wife or son or daughter or mother or father. Perhaps you lost your job this year. Or you've received a diagnosis that has left you staggering. Perhaps in your pain you're wondering where God is. Peace is absent from your life.

Oh, how we'd love to capture the wonder and joy and magic of that first Christmas and carry it around with us all the time! But the angels returned to heaven, the shepherds went back to work, the wise men returned to their country, the blazing star disappeared, and a jealous, insane king ordered the slaughter of all male children two and under.

In 1872 Longfellow's poem was set to music. Today we know it as "I Heard the Bells on Christmas Day." The last stanza reads: "Then pealed the bells more loud and deep: 'God is not dead, nor doth He sleep; The wrong shall fail, the right prevail With peace on earth, good will to men.'"

What a message of hope! Even in our deepest pain and grief and despair, the last candle burns: Immanuel. God is with us. Yesterday, today, and always.

As I light the center candle on my Advent wreath—the white candle—I am reminded that it symbolizes Jesus, your Son, who came to give us hope, love, joy, and peace. Thank you, God, for the best Christmas present of all. Amen.

MORE TEA: Read and meditate on Luke 2:1–20.

All I Want for Christmas

... making the most of the time ... –Ephesians 5:15 RSV

LEFTOVER TURKEY IN THE fridge. Blaze orange clothing over backs of chairs. Plastic bins of Christmas decorations in the hall. Has it really been a year since I packed them away? Before I know it, I'll be packing them up again.

Slow down, time, and let me savor each day as this season unfolds. Let me not get so caught up with lists and just the right gift and programs and housecleaning and baking, that by the time the day comes, I'll be a bah-humbug.

Do you know what I've wanted to do for a long time?

Toss the lists—we have too much already. Closets and drawers overflowing. Food getting moldy in the fridge. Weight and health problems because we have over and above what we need and too many things we really don't want.

I'd like to give Christmas away. Take all that money I'd spend on gifts that no one really needs and give it to someone who does. I'd like to go Christmas shopping for a family who wouldn't have a Christmas otherwise. Food, clothes, toys. Pack it in boxes, leave it on their doorstep, ring the doorbell, and then hide and watch the wonder, the surprise, the joy.

But I'm locked in tradition. And I lack the courage to break it.

Maybe this year, though, I can make a start—by telling my family not to get me anything. I'm not being a martyr here. Honest. I have more than enough.

And ask them, instead, for time. Time to enjoy a leisurely meal together. And it doesn't have to be one someone spent all day in the kitchen preparing. Macaroni and cheese or bought pizza would be just fine. Time to watch a movie together and eat popcorn. Time to sit around the table and talk or play Monopoly or Sorry or Uno Attack. So what if my twenty-three-year-old son tromps me by fifty points every time we play Scrabble?

I want to call Sam and Deb and invite them to, as they so often joked, "come visit the poor folks."

I don't want to look back, at the end of my life, and cry, like poor, rich Solomon did, "Meaningless! Meaningless! Everything was meaningless!" (Ecclesiastes 1:2).

The most meaningful gifts don't come with a price tag.

Like time. Like sharing. Like love. Like family. After all, when the chips are down, who else do we have? As Robert Frost once wrote, "Home is the place where, when you have to go there, they have to take you in."*

In the end, it all comes down to choice.

"Two roads diverged in a wood, and I—I took the one less traveled by, and that has made all the difference." *

Dear God, give me the courage to take the road less traveled by. Amen.

*"The Death of the Hired Man" and "The Road Not Taken" by Robert Frost.

MORE TEA: Read and meditate on Matthew 25:31–46;
1 Corinthians 13.

The Mess the Magi Made

"Where is the one who has been born king of the Jews?" –Matthew 2:2 NIV

IT WAS AN INNOCENT enough question. But what ramifications! Who would have known?

As a child I simply accepted the story of the three kings who brought gifts of gold, frankincense, and myrrh to the Christ child. But as an adult I now see not just the miracle of the star, the mysterious appearance of the Magi (who weren't really kings, but literally *magoi*, "wise men"), and the lavish gifts. I also see the mess they created when they made a stop in Jerusalem to ask directions.

"Where is the one who has been born king of the Jews?" they asked the natives. "We saw his star in the East and have come to worship him" (Matthew 2:2).

King Herod heard about it and sent for them. How were they to know Herod was a ruthless, power-hungry monarch whose list of murder victims included his wife, three sons, mother-in-law, brother-in-law, and uncle? Herod had no intention of worshiping the newborn king, as he told them.

After obtaining information they needed, the Magi left for Bethlehem, and what do you know—there was the star again. And it led them straight to the house where Jesus was.

That's what confuses me: why they had to stop and ask in the first place, if they were following the star. One of my commentaries states that "the star which they saw in the east now *reappeared* to act as a guide from Jerusalem to Bethlehem."

The story we hear every Christmas has the Magi following the star all the way from the East. Maybe they didn't. Maybe they saw it in their native country months earlier when Jesus was born, knew its significance, and headed west to pay homage to the newborn king.

That would explain why they had to stop and ask the natives about something they thought they should know.

What they didn't know is that because of their questions, Herod ordered the slaughter of all male children under the age of two who lived in Bethlehem and the surrounding territories.

Ever feel like you're in the middle of a mess you didn't create or that you innocently blundered into? That no matter what you do, you'll be the bad guy?

Sin does two things: it separates us from God, and it produces evil in the world. The first of these was taken care of at Calvary.

The second, well, look around. Even the innocent are hurt by what sin does.

But this is the real story of Christmas: the forgiveness God extended to man when that baby grew up and offered Himself as a sacrifice for our sins. And the hope that He will redeem all the wrongs and make them right.

"The thief comes only to steal and kill and destroy," Jesus said. "I have come that they might have life, and have it to the full" (John 10:10 NIV).

"And in despair I bowed my head: 'There is no peace on earth,' I said, 'For hate is strong and mocks the song of peace on earth, good will to men.' Then pealed the bells more loud and deep: 'God is not dead, nor doth he sleep; The wrong shall fail, the right prevail, With peace on earth, good will to men'" (from "I Heard the Bells on Christmas Day" by Henry Wadsworth Longfellow, Public Domain).

Thank You, Father, that no matter how bad things are, there is always hope with You. Amen.

MORE TEA: Read and meditate on Matthew 2:1–18.

A Season to Believe

Therefore the Lord himself will give you a sign: The virgin will conceive and give birth to a son, and will call him Immanuel. –Isaiah 7:14 NIV

Nothing, you see, is impossible with God. –Luke 1:37 The Message

I MET SUE SWAN IN 1997 when I began a writers group in Punxsutawney. She and her family had recently moved to the area when her husband accepted a job as the director of a local ministry.

Sue was the answer to my prayers. I'd been writing and submitting my work, but I had much to learn about the craft of writing and the world of publishing. Even though I'd gotten several pieces published nationally and was a feature writer for the local newspaper, I felt like I was way out in left field, all alone without a clue what to do when the ball came to me.

Enter Sue Swan. She'd read my classified ad about a writers group I was starting and showed up at the first meeting. Not only was she a published author, but she was also a member of the board of directors for the St. Davids Christian Writers' Conference, held at Geneva College in Beaver Falls every June.

We became fast friends. She had much to offer, and I was so hungry to learn. We discovered we had much in common: faith, a love for tea and reading, a desire to serve God through our writing, and our birthday—November 5.

Sue was instrumental in me attending my first writing conference, nominating me for a scholarship to the St. Davids conference, which I received. I couldn't have afforded to attend otherwise. Eventually I became a member of the board of directors myself. Not only did I learn a great deal about writing and publishing, but I also made lifetime friendships.

Sue and her family eventually moved back to the Pittsburgh area. Her new job prevented her from staying involved with the St. Davids group, and we drifted out of touch. One year she showed up at the conference wearing an oxygen mask. A cylinder of the life-giving gas accompanied her wherever she went.

She'd been diagnosed with sarcoidosis, a chronic, progressive lung disease, which led to pulmonary arterial hypertension. There is no cure for either disease. Her only hope for her worsening condition was a lung transplant. Despite her prognosis, however, she remained cheerful and upbeat—and encouraging to others.

I continued to pray for her and receive updates, but the news was never good.

Until July 24, 2014—the day she was healed.

Yes, I said healed.

That was the day she and her husband, Tom, attended a breakfast session at the International Gideons Convention in

Philadelphia, and a man asked to pray for her. She consented. Here is what happened, in Sue's own words:

"I drew in a deep breath—and for the first time in ten years felt my lungs fully inflate. I took another deep breath with the same result. The constriction that had been getting progressively worse was gone. I jumped up, sobbing, laughing, and praising God. I threw my arms around Tom and said, 'I can breathe! Sweetheart, *I can breathe!*' "*

I saw Sue in October. She drove up from Pittsburgh for the Punxsutawney Christian Women's Conference and stayed with me overnight Saturday night. There is no sign of her illnesses.

Christmas is a season of miracles. Everything surrounding the birth of Jesus was miraculous: barren Elizabeth conceiving and bearing the forerunner of the Messiah; the appearances of angels to an old priest, an engaged young woman, a bewildered fiancé, and a group of shivering shepherds; a virgin birth; a wondrous star that guided three wise men from the East to the newborn baby; the escape of that baby from a crazed king.

You've read the story.

But it's more than a story. It's more than God reaching down and touching mankind, blessing us with a miracle.

It's God actually leaving the splendors of heaven to inhabit a human body and live with us on earth so He could provide the way for us to be with Him forever.

Christmas is the season we want to believe in miracles. So many need one now.

So go ahead—believe a miracle can happen. Believe in the impossible.

"We serve a God of power, love, and miracles," writes Sue. "I am living proof that miracles did not end with recorded Scripture. God is still sovereign and still delights in miraculously healing His children."

I do believe, Lord! Help me overcome my unbelief! (Mark 9:24) Amen.

NOTE: *Read Sue's story, "God Still Works Miracles," on her blog http://susanreithswan.com/2014/08/03/god-still-works-miracles-part-one/

The story is told in four parts, which include her miraculous healing, the story of the man who laid his hand on her head and prayed for her, her subsequent visits to her doctors, and other "God-incidences" surrounding this miracle.

MORE TEA: Read and meditate on Luke 1:26–38.

The Most Wonderful Time of the Year

The people walking in darkness have seen a great light; on those living in the land of deep darkness a light has dawned. –Isaiah 9:2 NIV

FOR THE PAST MONTH, folks have been complaining that Halloween decorations aren't even settled in their storage boxes when the Christmas lights are strung up, and Santa, Frosty, and Rudolph, as well as Nativity scenes, appear on lawns and porches. Christmas merchandise fills the store shelves by November 1, the date the Hallmark Movie Channel begins its "Countdown to Christmas" movies. I've read rants on Facebook telling people to "Wake up! It's only the beginning of November!"

I used to complain, too—mostly about the commercialization of a day that should be remembered and celebrated for the hope it brings humanity. I especially criticized the movies. This year, though, I've had a change of heart. Not about the commercialization—and I still say by the time Christmas comes I'll be sick of the "save Santa, save Christmas" movies.

I've changed my perspective on putting out decorations early—whatever you want to call early, because, really, isn't "early" relative? Early is whenever you think it's too early.

Me, I don't think putting out Christmas decorations in November is early. I would have had mine out, too, but DH (Dear Husband) has been busy preparing our place for winter. But now that Thanksgiving is past, I'm ready to deck the halls. The boxes and bins will come down from the attic, and by next weekend, my home will be adorned for Christmas.

Why the change of heart?

The Christmas season, like life, passes by much too quickly. It is, as the classic song goes, "the most wonderful time of the year." Why not stretch it out? Savor each day of the season as it unfolds. The best part of the journey is the anticipation of arriving at our destination. The fun is in the preparation.

And do look at preparing for Christmas as fun, not a tedious chore or something you're obligated to do. Have fun baking those cookies, signing those cards, wrapping those gifts. Inhale the joy. Let it expand into your being—into every fiber of your body, mind, heart, and soul.

Christmas isn't about presents or decorations or food or get-togethers. Those things are all part of the celebration of the arrival of the most wonderful gift God gave mankind—His Own Son, and with Him, the gift of hope.

The world may seem hopeless at times. Events—international, national, local, personal—may bring despair.

But during the Christmas season, we allow the Christmas lights, which symbolize the Light of the World, to cast out the darkness of despair and replace it with the light of hope. When we stretch out the Christmas season, we're extending a time of joy and hope and light and love.

So go ahead, put up those decorations as soon as you want to. Stretch out the most wonderful time of the year.

Thank you, Father, for the hope Christmas brings. Forgive us for our Grinch moments. Fill us with the spirit of the season. Amen.

MORE TEA: Read and meditate on John 1:1–14.

Angel in the Snow

Are not all angels ministering spirits sent to serve those who will in-herit salvation? –Hebrews 1:14 NIV

DO YOU BELIEVE IN angels—heavenly beings who pop in and out of our lives, unrecognized until we realize we've been touched by something divine?

Angels are mentioned throughout the Bible as far back as the Garden of Eden, acting as God's servants, protecting, nurtur-ing, giving messages from God. But it is with Christmas they are most associated. A flurry of angel activity accompanied the birth of baby Jesus in Bethlehem.

But that was more than two thousand years ago. Do angels really exist? Or are they simply characters in a charming story? And if they are real, do they appear today, in this modern, high-tech, sophisticated, cynical world?

Karen Bassaro of Clymer, Pennsylvania, believes they do. Here is her story:

"A miracle happened to us almost twenty-two years ago. I should say it happened to my son, Jason.

"We had bought an older home and were starting to remodel it. I can remember thinking, 'Life is so good. I have a good husband, a beautiful daughter, and a precious son.' Little did I know my life was about to change."

She'd decided to make french fries for supper but had to use the outlets in the dining room because they were remodeling the kitchen.

"I told my daughter to move some play things so Jason, who was a speed demon in his walker, wouldn't come near the counter where the deep fryer was. I no more than turned my back and Jason was at the counter with the fryer cord! I don't even know how he got it.

"He pulled the hot grease on himself. It was my worst nightmare. Not even one year old, and my son was life-flighted to the Mercy Hospital burn unit in Pittsburgh."

Thirty percent of Jason's little body had deep, second- and third-degree burns. Doctors told the Bassaros he would not live through the weekend.

"But he did," Karen said.

But the life-and-death struggle was far from over.

"Each day it was something new, from worrying about infection to being told he would not move his neck and arm again. So many prayers and Masses were said for him. We received cards and notes from family, friends, and strangers."

After six weeks, Jason returned home, one day before Christmas Eve.

"He was still a very sick little boy," Karen said. "But you could tell he was happy to be home."

The Bassaros learned to change his dressings and tend to his therapy. Determined that he would move his arm and neck again, Karen's husband played games with Jason to get him to move them.

"When it seemed like things were starting to look up, a trip to Pittsburgh crushed our hopes. The doctor told us Jason's scars would be bad and he might not ever have hair. I felt that sick, helpless feeling again.

"On the way home, my husband knew I needed to stop at a shrine I often prayed at. It was at this shrine of Mary that I felt God was right beside me.

"When we reached the shrine, a new blanket of snow had fallen. I was crying, so I didn't notice another car was also there. When we got out of the car, an older gentleman was on the steps. He said 'hello' to me, my husband, and my daughter. He said nothing to Jason.

"As I carried Jason up the steps, he gave Jason this warm, smiling look. My thought was to get to the top of the steps to pray.

"It was only when we started down the steps that we noticed the gentleman made no footprints in the snow, no tire tracks from where his car was.

"It was at that moment I knew God sent us an angel, a special angel to let us know Jason would be fine.

"From that moment on, Jason did everything the doctors said he wouldn't be able to. And now, years later, my son is a senior in college.

"Are there scars? Yes, a few, but Jason says that makes him who he is."

Karen describes Jason as "a handsome guy with a great personality and friends everywhere." And despite what doctors predicted, he does have hair.

"Will Jason make it in the world after college?" she concluded. "Oh, yes, he will. I know this because an angel on a snow-covered day told me so."

Father, remove the cynicism that has infected my soul and replace it with the childlike faith that believes in angels and miracles. Amen.

MORE TEA: Read and meditate on Matthew 1:18–2:20.

Miracle Baby

Call to me and I will answer you. –Jeremiah 33:3 NIV

IN HER BOOK, *God Just Showed Up*, Linda Watkins includes the story of a young pregnant drug addict who, in the middle of a drug-induced beating by her husband, turned to a God she wasn't sure was real.

Curled up in a ball to protect the baby in her womb, she prayed silently, "God, if You're real, please help me escape this hell."

Aloud, she cried to her husband, "Please stop!"

Amazingly, he did, offering her, instead of his fist, his crack pipe. Snatching it, she fled to the bathroom. Leaning on the sink to light the pipe, she felt her baby move.

"I gripped the pipe in one hand and my stomach in the other. At that moment, I had no idea which was more important."

She peered at her reflection in the mirror and shuddered at what she saw.

"Dark raccoon circles surrounded my sunken eyes. My skin was dry and old-looking, lips cracked. Dehydration was wasting me away. I looked down at the trickles of blood oozing from my ripped, throbbing skin and felt myself dying," she wrote.

"What am I turning into?" she asked herself.

Right there, she determined to flee. Then the contractions started. She managed to make it out the door without her husband noticing. Barefoot and in her robe, she flagged down a cab, which took her to the nearest hospital.

There, the doctor gave her little hope for the well-being of her baby, who was one month premature.

"Your baby is at a very high risk of being born with multiple complications," he said. "There could be deformity and mental retardation, and, definitely, this baby will experience withdrawal. How severe, we will just have to wait and see."

The son she bore, however, had none of the complications the doctors expected, not even withdrawal.

"Sugar," a nurse told her, "there must be a God in your corner."

Today, this woman is the founder and president of a ministry that provides self-awareness workshops and seminars for women. And that miracle baby, a teenager at the time this story was written, was an honors student, athlete, and an award-winning artist.

A miracle, something the laws of nature or science cannot explain, also happened to a young Jewish girl named Mary more than two thousand years ago. A virgin, she conceived and became pregnant, as was predicted by the prophet Isaiah hundreds of years earlier (Isaiah 7:14). That baby was the Son of God. Impossible? A miracle is God reaching down and making the impossible happen.

Are there prerequisites to qualify for a miracle? Do you have to be somebody big and important? Mary, in her spontaneous song of praise, known as the "Magnificat" (which means "glorifies"), said, "He has exalted the lowly" (Luke 1:52). Yes, God works miracles even for the lowest when they call to Him for help. "Call to me and I will answer you, and show you great and mighty things," He promises in Jeremiah 33:3.

Maybe a miracle requires great faith. After all, didn't Mary have great faith when she said to the angel, "Let it be done to me according to your word" (Luke 1:38)? Yet, the young woman in this story did not have great faith when she called to God. Faith the size of a mustard seed will do (Matthew 17:20), faith enough to try one more time when you've come up empty time after time (Luke 5:1–11), to step out into the storm and walk on water (Matthew 14:28).

You need only to believe, even with a scrap of faith, that there *is* a God and He wants to help you. All you have to do is ask.

Dear God, sometimes my mustard seed is shriveled. I've become too cynical. Help me to grow a faith that will move mountains. Amen.

MORE TEA: Read and meditate on Luke 1:26–56.

The Year We Couldn't Afford Christmas

"THERE WON'T BE ANY gifts under the tree this year," my mother announced about a week before Christmas in 1962. "In fact, there won't even be a tree. We don't have the money."

I was eleven years old. My brother Pete was fifteen, and my sister Judy, fourteen. Two years earlier my father had lost his job at the local steel mill, and our family of five went from being haves to have-nots. Suppers became meatless fares, often with only one item on the menu. A roll of toilet paper replaced the tissue on top of the metal cabinet in the kitchen.

The timing of the layoff—a result of the 1959 recession— couldn't have been worse. My parents had just taken out a loan to pay for a rustic vacation cabin in the western Pennsylvania mountains, three hours to the north of our home in the Mon Valley. Jobs for a fifty-year-old carpenter were scarce. So Dad took a civil service exam and landed a position as a state building inspector, but his office was a four-hour drive away on treacherous mountain roads. He lived in motels and boarding houses, with expenses coming out of his pocket, and came home once a month.

I don't remember anything else my mother said that day. I just remember thinking, "What can I do?" While I could accept that there would be no presents, I couldn't imagine a Christmas without a tree.

That weekend Mother Nature helped us out by blanketing the valley with inches and inches of wet, heavy snow. That was before snow blowers and home tractors with plows. All we had were shovels.

Without telling anyone, I went around the neighborhood, shoveling snow off sidewalks and coins into my coat pocket. Later that day, I emptied my pockets on the kitchen table.

"Here, Mom," I said, hope welling up within me. "I hope this is enough for a tree."

It wasn't. But later that day a Christmas tree appeared on our front porch.

"How . . . ?" I asked my mother.

"Your brother went out and shoveled driveways," she said, dark brown eyes glistening like the snow outside. How many driveways he had to shovel to get enough, I have no idea, but it was no easy task for a skinny teenage boy whose passion was music, not sports.

But there were more surprises that year: gifts under the tree. Pete had made enough that day to buy my sister and me each a pajama bag, as well as a gift for Mom and Dad. In addition, he gave the $25 he had left to Mom.

You've heard it said that Christmas isn't about gifts.

I beg to differ. Christmas *is* about gifts.

In 1962 a scrawny teenage boy from a family that couldn't afford Christmas gave more than a Christmas tree and presents of pajamas for his sisters. He gave his heart—and this sister, more than fifty years later, considers that the best gift she's ever received.

Thank you, God, for teaching me early on what a true gift is. Amen.

MORE TEA: Read and meditate on John 3:16.

Miscellaneous

For everything there is a season.

–Ecclesiastes 3:1 ESV

Blarney, Baloney, or Ballyhoo
St. Patrick's Day

The grass withers and the flowers fade, but the word of our God endures forever. –Isaiah 40:8 NIV

ON ST. PATRICK'S DAY, IT seems, everyone is Irish.

We love the story of the man who supposedly drove out the snakes from Ireland and used a shamrock, with its three leaves, to teach the Irish about the Trinity.

We do love our heroes, and we do love our holidays, don't we? But how often do we stop and think about the holiday we're celebrating? Or do a little research into the real life of the hero?

We associate St. Patrick and the shamrock with Ireland.

But in reality, he was actually the son of wealthy Roman citizens who was kidnapped as a teenager and taken to Ireland, where he was sold as a slave. Like Moses and David of old, Patrick spent his days and nights on a lonely mountainside watching his master's sheep, often in brutal conditions.

After six years, he escaped and returned home, no longer the spoiled and rebellious teenager he was when he was abducted.

Instead of assuming a life of privilege as his family expected, he felt called to return to Ireland, this time as a missionary. The rest, as they say, is history. Or legend. Or myth.

Actually, there were no snakes in Ireland for Patrick to banish. Except the snakes of paganism, superstition, petty Irish rulers, and religious leaders who jealously guarded their turf. And the shamrock? According to one of Ireland's leading botanists, "Shamrocks exist only on St. Patrick's Day. Every other day of the year, it's known simply as young clover."

Over time symbolism evolved into story, which we too often accept as fact. But the beauty of the legend of St. Patrick isn't in the myths we celebrate. It's in the true story of the transcendent purpose and transforming power of God in Patrick's life.

You see, it was on that desolate mountain that young Patrick found God and his true purpose in life.

Funny how God uses the hard times to get our attention. And change our lives. And transform us, molding us into the vision He has for each of us.

Are you enduring hard times?

Hang in there and work with God. He has allowed this time for a reason.

My friend and sister-in-Christ Lillie often reminds me of God's view on our difficulties: " 'For I know the plans I have for you,' declares the LORD. 'Plans to prosper you and not to harm you, plans to give you hope and a future'" (Jeremiah 29:11 NIV).

We have to sift through legends and myths to discover the germ of truth in them, but we can take God at His Word.

And that's no blarney!

Lord, it can be so confusing, living in this world, trying to discern what is true and what is false, what is fact and what is embellished story. Remind me to cling to Your Word in times of doubt, knowing that You never lie. Amen.

MORE TEA: Read and meditate on Psalm 19.

Fools and Fun
April Fools' Day

The fool says in his heart, "There is no God." –*Psalm 14:1 NIV*

A BRITISH TELEVISION STATION once broadcast a documentary about "spaghetti farmers" and how they harvested their crop from "spaghetti trees." The film, however, was an elaborate April Fools' Day joke and wasn't to be taken seriously.

The harmless pranks played on the unsuspecting, such as telling someone his shoe is untied or a spider is in her hair, are all in fun, and falling victim to an April Fools' Day joke doesn't mean you're a fool, but that you've been fooled. There's a difference.

A fool, by definition, is someone who lacks common sense and wisdom. These are the people for whom the day is named.

Until 1582 the New Year was observed around the spring equinox, at the end of March, with an eight-day celebration that culminated on April 1. But with the introduction of the Gregorian calendar, New Year's Day was moved to January 1. Back in those days, communication was slow, and it took several years before everyone was on the same page.

Some, however, adamantly refused to change and continued to celebrate the New Year on April 1. These stubborn folks were called fools and became the target of mean-spirited jokes meant to harass them.

Being a fool is no fun and is dangerous to your spiritual health. In biblical times, calling someone a fool was the worst thing you could say about him.

According to God's Word, a fool is a person who doesn't believe in God, refuses to be taught, hates knowledge, has a quick temper and a quicker tongue, is impulsive and reckless, doesn't take sin seriously, spreads slander, doesn't learn from his mistakes, trusts in himself, insists he's right, isn't money-smart, despises discipline, refuses to correct what's wrong, and is a bad influence.

Today, even with an explosion of knowledge at our fingertips, fools abound. A fool isn't someone who lacks knowledge but rather one who refuses to use it.

The remedy for foolishness is wisdom, and all we need to know in order to be wise is found in God's Word. Reading it, meditating on it, and applying it to our lives prevents one from being an April Fool all year round.

Dear God, sometimes I act like a fool. Give me the desire to read Your Word consistently and absorb it so that I may be wise. Amen.

MORE TEA: Read and meditate on Matthew 7:24–27.

That's America!
Independence Day

Blessed is the nation whose God is the LORD. —Psalm 33:12 NIV

EVERY TIME I GO to town, I pass the Rossiter baseball field. And I think, "Now, that's America!"

Let me tell you why.

Every spring, dedicated volunteers clean up and ready the fields for the season. Before every game, the infield is raked, the baselines limed, and the bases put in place. Between games the outfield grass is kept clipped and neat.

Volunteers—you'll find them everywhere, in hospitals, libraries, historical societies, and on Little League fields. As I think of this powerful force that helps to keep things running better and more smoothly, I think, "Now, that's America!"

Each year improvements are made to the ball field area: new bleachers, a playground, a port-a-potty, a picnic pavilion, and a lighted flagpole atop which Old Glory flies day and night, have been added. Facing the bleachers is an old-fashioned scoreboard, where someone keeps the runs tallied as runners cross the plate.

Sponsors' signs hang on the chain-link fence surrounding the field.

Last fall heavy rains flooded the small town of less than a thousand and damaged the outfield fence. Then, a couple of winters ago, the section of fence near the road came down due to either heavy snow or an out-of-control vehicle. All repairs were made before the season started.

I think of these local business owners who dip into their pockets, even in trying economic times, to donate needed cash for the upkeep of the "Field of Dreams," and I think, "Now, that's America!"

Folks watch the games from their porches across the road and in the shade on the hill on the third base side—across the creek where foul balls often splash and kids scramble to retrieve them. Canvas chairs fill up the spectators' area as game time nears. I think of baseball fans that fill the bleachers in every town across America to cheer on sons, grandsons, nephews, neighbors, and the teams they love, and I think, "Now, that's America!"

Rossiter was born in 1901 during the coal boom era in western Pennsylvania. For the longest time, a stark black mountain of residue left from the mines shadowed the ball field, the first thing I'd see coming down the hill into this former coal mining town. But that ugly landmark has since been removed, replaced by the verdant hillside where fans watch the games in the shade of trees and set off noisemakers when the Miners score a home run.

The Rossiter ball team named themselves for the men who made their living in the bowels of the earth and whose families grew the town that has survived even though the mines shut down in the late 1940s. I think of folks like these, who eke out a living during boom times and bust times, and survive and grow, and I think, "Now, that's America!"

Down the street from the ball field is a relatively new building—built on the ground where the Rossiter School once stood. American Legion Post 582. And I think of the men and women who have served this country down through the years, from the signing of the Declaration of Independence to the fighting of Communism and terrorists across the globe, and I think, "Now, that's America!"

Thank you, God, for this wonderful country and the men and women who make it what it is. Amen.

MORE TEA: Read and meditate on Psalm 33.

Memorial Stones
September 11

These stones are to be a memorial to the people of Israel forever. –
Joshua 4:7 NIV

SEPTEMBER 11, 2001, DAWNED clear and bright. Fall was in
the air—in the coolness of the misty morning, in the hints of
red, yellow, and orange beginning to splash the hillsides, in the
honking of geese winging overhead. America shut off the alarm
clock, rolled out of bed, opened the curtains, and let in the day.
With coffee in hand, we set off to work.

By nine a.m. our world had profoundly, irreversibly
changed. By noon we'd gone from disbelief to numbing shock.
By evening we vowed, "We will not forget!"

And we haven't. One of the most tragic days in American history was also one of our finest. We looked in the mirror on that
watershed day and said, "We are America." And then we
showed the world what makes America the greatest nation on
earth.

America is a land of opportunity. We still open our arms to
the tired, poor, huddling masses yearning to breathe free. To
those homeless, tempest-tossed souls, the lamp is still lifted be-

side the golden door. In every community modern-day immigrants practice medicine, serve cultural cuisine, sell cars. Some are so desperate they sneak in. Don't let anyone fool you. Opportunities abound in the home of the brave. But that isn't what makes America great.

America is a land of prosperity. We have houses for our cars. We have closets jam-packed with clothes we grew out of or that we forgot we owned. We have winter clothes and summer clothes. We have footwear for every occasion. We have everyday dishes and good dishes. We have bank accounts, credit cards, investments, retirement plans. We have boats and swimming pools and RVs and motorcycles and four-wheelers and garages so full of stuff that we don't have room for the car. We eat three square meals a day and then some. Diet and exercise businesses are booming. But our material wealth isn't what makes America great.

America is the land of the free. We work and still have time to play. We race cars and horses and the clock. We are free to worship and work where we choose. We are free from want and, for the most part, from fear. We have homeless shelters and Homeland Security. We have soup kitchens and supersonic jets. We have policemen, firemen, EMTs, the Red Cross, the Salvation Army, and the military protecting and aiding us. We can be whatever we want to be, go where we want to go. We can choose who, what, when, where, and how. We have life, liberty, and the pursuit of happiness. But freedom isn't what makes America great.

What, then, makes America great?

Its generous heart, resilient spirit, and can-do attitude. The Spirit of America born on the shores of Plymouth Rock nearly four centuries ago was found on September 11, 2001, in the rubble that was the World Trade Center and in the wreckage of a plane that slammed into a Pennsylvania field.

On a memorial stone, those stalwart Pilgrims inscribed: "This spot marks the final resting place of the Pilgrims of the *Mayflower*. In weariness and hunger and in cold, fighting the wilderness and burying their dead in common graves that the Indians should not know how many had perished, they here laid the foundations of a state for which all men for countless ages should have liberty to worship God in their own way. All ye who pass by and see this stone, remember, and dedicate yourselves anew to the resolution that you will not rest until this lofty ideal shall have been realized throughout the earth."

We will not forget September 11, 2001. We will not forget that, for a moment, evil prevailed. We will not forget how, by the grace of God, we rolled up our sleeves and went to work, fighting that evil with goodness. We will not forget who and what we are. Let our memorial stones reflect the spirit of America.

God, bless America, land that I love. Amen.

MORE TEA: Read and meditate on Joshua 4:1–9, 20–24.

Remember the Forgotten
Veterans Day

There is no greater love than to lay down one's life for one's friends.
–John 15:13 NLT

MY COUSIN MARY ANN'S career as a military nurse was the inspiration for my second novel, *The Heart Remembers*.

While my cousin served at a US Navy hospital in Japan during the Vietnam War years, Vangie, the main character in my novel, was a fictional Army nurse who served during that conflict. Vietnam, specifically Pleiku, a town in the central highlands, was the setting for Part One of the book. However, the story wasn't about the war. The war was but a backdrop of the romance between Vangie and Seth, a medical evacuation helicopter pilot.

Through my research, I pored through several books, including *A Piece of My Heart* by Keith Walker and *Home Before Morning* by Lynda Van Devanter, true stories of military nurses who'd served in Vietnam. I learned of the Army's medical evacuation program in *Rescue Under Fire: The Story of Dust Off in Vietnam* by

John Cook. I read about the bravery of Dust Off pilot Chief Warrant Officer Michael J. Novosel that earned him a Medal of Honor. I learned of the Medcap program that provided medical care to the Qui Hoa Leper Hospital.

In short, I discovered there was good done in Vietnam that never saw press.

The Heart Remembers is a story that patriotic me wrote with passion and sorrow. I was a high school, then college student during the Vietnam War years. I knew of the protests and the shameful treatment the Vietnam veterans received when they returned stateside. Not a hero's welcome, that's for sure.

I hoped my book would somewhat right the wrong by showing at least a glimpse of the courage, grit, and compassion shown in the midst of a very unpopular war. I'm not saying everything done in Vietnam was humane. But since when is war, at any time, humane? When is any war a "popular" war?

When the manuscript was finished, a local Vietnam veteran who was a former Navy Seal read it for accuracy. Then I sent it off. Several publishers seriously considered it. A senior acquisitions editor for a major Christian publishing house liked it so much she presented the manuscript to the committee that determines what gets published and what doesn't. I had high hopes.

Until I received her email: "Our editorial board met yesterday, and I regret to say we won't be moving ahead with *The Heart Remembers*. There was still a lot of concern about the salability of the Vietnam War even as a partial setting, and I'm sorry about that."

"Even after all these years," I told my husband, "these poor Vietnam vets are still getting slammed."

So I published it myself as an independent author–publisher.

The Heart Remembers stands as my tribute to the brave men and women who served their country during a war that some folks still try to hide in the closet. Yet the Vietnam vets I know proudly fly Old Glory in their front yards.

Every Veteran' Day, this heart remembers.

Thank you, Lord, for the selfless men and women who have served and are serving their country. Bless them and protect them. Smile upon them and be gracious to them. Show them Your favor and give them Your peace (Numbers 6:24–26 NLT). Amen.

MORE TEA: Read and meditate on John 15:9–17.

ABOUT THE AUTHOR

MICHELE HUEY is an award-winning author whose published books include several novels, as well as compilations from her award-winning newspaper column. Her favorite setting for her fiction is western Pennsylvania, where she lives with her husband, Dean, who provides her with much fodder for her writing. The mother of three grown children and the grandmother of nine, she loves hiking, camping, swimming, and reading, and is an avid (and sometimes rabid) Pittsburgh Pirates fan. Visit Michele online at michelehuey.com.

BOOKS BY MICHELE HUEY

FICTION

The Heart Remembers
Mid-LOVE Crisis (formerly *Before I Die*)
Getaway Mountain: PennWoods Mystery Book 1

COMING SOON

Ghost Mountain: PennWoods Mystery Book 2

DEVOTIONAL

Minute Meditations: Meeting God in Everyday Experiences
I Lift Up My Eyes: Minute Meditations Vol. 2
God, Me & a Cup of Tea
God, Me & a Cup of Tea for the Seasons

Look for these titles on Amazon in Kindle and paperback formats.

CONTACT INFORMATION

Email: michelehueybooks@gmail.com

Website: michelehuey. com

Blog: godmetea. com

You'll also find me on Goodreads, Facebook, Twitter, Google Plus, LinkedIn, Instagram, and Pinterest. Connect with me!

Dear Reader,

I hope you enjoyed *God, Me & a Cup of Tea for the Seasons*. Please consider submitting a review and/or rating on Amazon and Goodreads (goodreads.com/michelehuey). Your feedback is greatly appreciated.

Blessings,
Michele

Made in the USA
Middletown, DE
12 November 2022

14759823R00195